Spectrum

Royal Palm Beach Writers

is proud to present this book
to the reading public.

ENJOY!

Dedication

This volume of literary offerings is dedicated to all writers, would-be writers, and readers who have a passion for the written word.

Acknowledgments

Royal Palm Beach Writers is sponsored by the Village of Royal Palm Beach, Florida.

We thank Mayor Pinto and the Village Council for their continued support and encouragement. All proceeds from the sale of this book will be returned to the Village.

We extend our heartfelt appreciation to Virginia Guido, for her invaluable dedication and care in the preparation, and Karina Felix for the layout and cover artwork of this issue of *Spectrum* Volume 14.

Spectrum is a collection of original writing from members of Royal Palm Beach Writers.

The **stories, essays,** and **poems** in this anthology are extensions of personal imagination, with some of the pieces derived from monthly writing prompts. Thus, a few segments might have similar titles or themes. In those instances, we hope you'll enjoy reading these like-minded elements of creativity, dreams, and fantasies.

Spectrum

Royal Palm Beach Writers

Short Stories, Essays, Poems, Fiction, Non-fiction
www.RoyalPalmBeachWriters.com

Library of Congress Cataloging-in-Publication Data

ISBN-13: 978-1-7329696-0-5

Printed in the United States of America
Cover Design by: Virginia Guido and Karina G. Felix
Illustration by: Karina G. Felix
Published by: Ingenious Publishers Inc.
www.IngeniousPublishers.com

The paper used in this publication meets the minimum requirements of the American National Standards for information Sciences – Permanence of Paper for Printed Library Material.

In Memory of

Jim Wiggins

March 30,1930 - September 9, 2018

Table of Contents

SOMEONE LIKE YOU

Virginia Guido

Why am I inspired to write? Do I feel I have a better story to tell than others before me? Not really. Is there a message I wish to convey to poor lost souls like me?

Yes! Like me, those unfortunate ones who are living on the edge of groups, cliques, or clubs because "you just don't fit in" need reassurance of their exceptional existence. Do we want to fit in? Should we adjust our psyche to satisfy others, or can we be unique without people judging us?

That's my purpose for writing my stories: to put into words the distressing feelings we experience when we discover our life-styles, upbringing, and status are different from society's idea of normal and not accepted, just tolerated.

If the pen is mightier than the sword, (thank you, Shake-speare), then the pen could also be the balm that heals broken hearts. I'm inspired to articulate, in print, what others are thinking, allowing them to embrace their diversity, thus becoming the salve that mends minds.

I'm motivated to highlight my own personal stories, letting others know that it's okay to think outside the box, live outside the box, or even design your own damned box! Display that box as a representation of your own creation. Do it with pride.

Can't meet the full criteria of the popular social group?

Make your own group popular, because we are not flying solo in this world. We are the creative beings, intelligent, energetic, yet misunderstood.

Will I pen "The Great American Novel"? Not likely, but maybe, just maybe, one lonely depressed reader will peruse my work and say, "That's me! I can relate to her words and I'm not alone after all."

Yes, I am inspired to write by the delusion that I might help someone else pick up her self-esteem, celebrate her differences, and not settle for anyone or any group who won't accept her, acknowledge who she is, or welcome her uniqueness.

Someone like me.

AND IF JOHNNY CAN'T READ

Jim Wiggins

And if Johnny can't read, let him know the ways of life in passing so that he may know right from wrong.

Destroy not his trust in humanity, nor his quest for truth or creativity.

May he not feel alone in the world, but grant him the ability to feel confident in his aloneness and serenity in feeling right with himself.

When his eyes fail to transmit the sounds of vowels or consonants, may he still be able to discern truth from falsehood.

Though lacking in decoding sounds upon the page, let him hear with clarity the songs of the mockingbird and to appreciate the rhythmic choir of birds on wing and the sound of a babbling stream.

Grant him the ability to decipher the colors of a rainbow and stand in awe of a sunrise or sunset. Allow him to marvel at the laws of nature and do his part in helping to preserve it.

And if Johnny can't read, let him not be ashamed even though the letters on a Scrabble board may seem scrambled in his mind. Do not destroy his belief in the harmony of all that has been created holy and good, including life itself.

May he feel content within himself, awakening each day with a sense of happiness in knowing that he is special.

ON WRITING

Richard Paul Angelini

Let the million-dollared ride!
Barefoot, trudging at his side,
Thou hast more than he can buy
In the reach of ear and eye, -
Outward sunshine, inward joy:
Blessings on thee, barefoot boy!

Excerpt from The Barefoot Boy by John Greenleaf Whittier

The barefoot boy running, the solitary fisherman balancing the forces of nature, the old woman cautiously crossing the street, incidents that all challenge what may come. Our literature attempts to attract and then capture the essence of being, the incident, the challenge.

Is it the happy trudging that makes the challenge? The size of the fish? The busy street? Alone, they are only sights. Perhaps a glancing observation or two. What in the character makes the writer turn his head and really see? Want to tell you? And yet, stop and ponder before putting into ink profound emotions that are constantly changing as they write?

How do we penetrate the incident, challenge, character? Discover truths? Falsehoods?

The writing is an adventure. An adventure whose ending we cannot foretell. It is an adventure into ourselves in which we find the reason for incident and the reason for the character's action. For: *"what is character but the determination of incident? What is incident but the illustration of character?"* (Henry James)

Will the reader take only an inquisitive look? Or has the writer captured the character's most intimate action with incident, and put it on paper? Will the reader *"cross the line... between performing for ... amusement, and cherishing the inescapable intimacy between self and the world?"* (Maud Pierre-Charles)

TALKING TO THE BLUES

Hartley Barnes

Give me some blues to rock my soul,
taking me through the nights
when loneliness is all I have.
Give me some blues to rock my soul,
taking me through the nights
when loneliness is all I have.

Those are lines from a blues song I never completed, a song I'd hoped to make famous, putting me on an easy street where there are no blues. The words would not come, and the few that did made no sense. I had the blues trying to write the blues.

Dig deep, deep, deep, until words gush from the trenches of my mind, and sync with the strings of the guitar, the heartbeat of the bass, and the thumping of the drums, I heard myself saying. That was not (preordained); the blues would not let me in. What secrets is it protecting? What does it not want me to know?

The blues frustrated me. The blues shunned me, saying, I don't have time to make anyone contented.

Soothe me with some lyrics to motivate my body to move with agility, pepping me up, and pulling me out of the furrow I'm mired in. Why are you being so elusive? I deserve to feel your blue ways; you are not exclusive to blues singers. The blues I want are not melancholy; that's the problem. You don't know how to be blissful. Admit you can't gratify my desire to quench the fire in me for peace of mind.

The blues I'm seeking is not about being cheated, betrayed, empty pockets, lack of love, or who is coming through the back door. The opposite of what— you are about— is what I want.
Be audacious and expose the other side of your coin where there are good things to be had, to revere, and to laugh at.

Send me something outside the box, filtering it through my ears for me to assimilate and to pass on to friends and foes.
I want good blues, not negatives. Talk to me with shades of delight and riffs to inspire the spirit. Dispel the notion that blues have to be . . . blue . . . blue . . . blue.

THE MURDER OF MX-133

Don Conway

Mr. Dillingworth murdered his robot, MX-133. He drowned it in the bathtub. Mr. Dillingworth's son, Robert, should have been able to predict the murder. After all, he was the director of the Robotics Laboratory at the Massachusetts Institute of Technology. When Robert became aware of his father's deteriorating mental condition, he thought MX-133 was ready for a field trial as caretaker for a human. MIT's Board of Directors was concerned about their liability if anything went wrong with the field trial. However, Robert convinced them that MX-133 was safe and ready and that this field trial would save many months in getting MX-133 ready for commercial production. The prospect of getting MX-133 on the market before anyone else and gaining domination in the Robotic Home Helper market was too tempting for the Board to pass up, so they gave him permission to take MX-133 home for a three months test.

The MX-133, now affectionately called Max, was programmed to handle the elder Mr. Dillkingworth's medication schedule, to prepare his favorite meals, do the laundry and general housework. Knowing of his father's curmudgeonly nature, Robert took great care in programming Max's human-interaction programs. To the casual observer, Max would appear to be the ultimate butler, housekeeper, handyman and companion for the eighty-five-year-old Mr. Dillingworth.

The day Robert brought Max home he sensed some tension between his father and the robot, but he attributed it to the newness and novelty of having a robot in the house. He was confident that with time, and Max's human-like programs, things would sort themselves out. They did not. For Mr. Dillingworth it was hate at first sight, but he hid his emotions because he was aware of the importance of the Field Trial to Robert's career.

During the first month of the trial, there seemed to be an uneasy truce between Max and Mr. Dillingworth. Signs of friction began to surface during the second month. It started with the medications. The old man resented being told that it, "is time for your pills." repeatedly until the pills were swallowed. At first, he tried to fool Max by putting the pills in his mouth but not swallowing them. Max soon caught on and demanded that Mr. Dillingworth open his mouth for a visual inspection.

Then came the arguments over food. Not only was Max a poor cook but he refused to cook with salt. He said he was not programmed for its use. The old man demonstrated four or five times how he wanted his clothes folded. The variety was too much for Max, so he ended up just rolling everything up and stuffing it into a draw.

The final break came when Max turned off the television at 8:00 p.m. and insisted it was bedtime for the old man.

Mr. Dillingworth's dislike for Max grew from hatred to thoughts of murder. It took him a while to come up with the idea of drowning the robot. He did several dry runs to get Max to climb into the bathtub. Max complained that it was Mr. Dillingworth who was supposed to get into the tub, not him. Arguments ensued, but in the end, the human won out, and Max obeyed; all the time insisting that, what Mr. Dillingworth wanted was "not logical."

On the afternoon of the murder, Mr. Dillingworth ordered Max to get into the tub. When the old man turned on the water, Max panicked and tried to climb out of the rising water. It was as if he knew what was going to happen to him. To thwart the robots attempts Mr. Dillingworth got into the tub and sat on Max's chest until the water completely covered the robot. MX-133 twisted and turned. His arms and legs began to twitch, and there were several small blue electric flashes. At that point, Mr. Dillingworth got out of the tub and stood looking down at the robot until the twitching stopped and there were no more electrical flashes. He left the body in the tub for two days

Television, and other Media all over the world, picked up the story of the murder. It was publicized as earth shattering and precedent setting in that it would determine the legal status of robots worldwide and for generations to come.

In the ensuing trial, the lawyers for MIT claimed that due to Max's many human-like characteristics, the crime was premeditated murder. They argued that if the death penalty was not imposed on the old man, then he should, at least, be sentenced to life imprisonment without the possibility of parole.

The defense lawyer argued two points on behalf of his client. They were that:

(1) the old man suffered from dementia and, (2) that, de-

spite the prosecutor's claim of Max's human-like characteristics, no actual human life was taken.

The judge's instructions to the jury were that they had firstly to decide whether or not Max should be considered as a human and, depending on that decision, the jury then had to give its recommendation for the form of punishment.

The jury deliberated for three days and then sent word to the judge that they were ready to announce their verdict.

Spectators and a hundred or more media personnel packed the courtroom when the jury filed in. The judge called for silence and then addressed the foreman of the jury, "Ladies and gentlemen of the jury, have you reached a verdict?" When the foreman stood up, the onlookers and media people fell silent and held their collective breaths. The foreman turned to face the judge and responded "Yes your honor we have."

"And what is your verdict?" the judge asked.

"We find the defendant….."

TO THE BEES

Donna S. Fernandez

I live among nobility.
I live with Royal Power.
I live alongside a Lilliputian livestock 120,000 strong.
Bees are peaceful.
Bees are beguiling.
I am beholden to them.

MY JOB HAS BEEN OUTSOURCED

Gloria H. Ferrara

I am proud to say that I am a lady of leisure; no longer do I have to be up at the crack of dawn to wake the sleepy, grumpy, toussled-hair student, whose first words upon opening one bleary eye are incoherent. He stumbled to be first in the bathroom--beating out my husband each morning.

My happiest moment of the morning, breakfast, need not be made, it never was consumed anyway. Of course, being the frugal person I am, it was my duty to eat it instead.
So, what if I had to jog for five miles each day to compensate for eating two breakfasts?
The exercise and fresh air amply replaced any belly fat that crept up as the years passed.

My job was outsourced from reminding toussled- hair student to be sure to take along any homework, be sure to go to piano lessons on the way home from school, be careful riding the bike, and when he got a car, to drive carefully.

My college student has moved out. I have passed on the mantle to him. Wake-up time, homework time, eating breakfast, are all his responsibilities now. From his weekly phone calls, I am assured he is doing fine. Wake-up time, reminders of homework, and even breakfast each morning are now well established in his new home. He lives off campus in a house he shares with boys and girls. He tells me they get along smoothly. Especially one special girl who, without any complaining, wakes him each morning, makes breakfast, and reminds him of any assignment he needs for the day.

College, they say, makes a man out of a boy. I'm still chewing that idea over, and after my morning run, day at the spa, lunch with the girls, dinner with my husband (who cooks anymore?) and monthly weekends visits with my son, I am glad to have had my job outsourced.

THE TWINS

D.M. Littlefield

Rose and Lilly Hanover, sixty-year-old spinster twin daughters of the town's founding father, looked exactly alike. They always dressed in identical clothes and wore their gray hair in the same style. The twins had lived together since childhood in their old Victorian mansion.

The only difference between them was their personalities. Rose was an extrovert and a person who liked being in charge. She was the proud principal of Hanover's grammar school, president of four women's organizations, and involved in all the town's clubs and functions.

Lilly, a librarian for the Hanover library, was an introvert. She was well educated, loved reading, and was content to stay in the background.

Today, they waited in line at the bank to give their accounts of the robbery. Rose glanced at her watch and tapped her toe. Frowning, she turned around to Lilly, who always stood behind her, and ranted, "I didn't know this was going to take so long. I don't want to be late for my women's club luncheon and my garden club meeting."

Rose waved at Detective Davis, who stood at the head of the line interviewing witnesses. When he glanced at her, she tapped her watch. "How long is this going to take?"

He rolled his eyes at the town's prima donna. "Be patient, Miss Hanover, I'll get to you soon."

Rose grumbled, "Listen, Lilly, I need to go. Tell that detective that the bank robber is about thirty years old, six feet tall, overweight, and not clean shaven. He has green eyes, and long, dark-brown oily hair that needs a shampoo." She huffed. "I don't know why men wear their hair that long nowadays. Short hair looks better." Rose poked Lilly. "Pay attention! His complexion was clear, except for a small scar on his left cheek. He was wearing black pants and a pale-blue shirt that was unbuttoned four buttons down from his neck. He wore a gold lion's-head ring on the third finger of his callused right hand. Oh, and he had dirty shoes." Rose rushed away before Lilly could utter a protest.

It was another thirty minutes before it was Lilly's turn to be interviewed. Detective Davis smiled and asked, "Miss Hanover, what can you tell me about the bank robber?"

Lilly glanced around uneasily and brought a shaky hand to her forehead. She cleared her throat a few times and stared at her feet before she blurted, "Um, he, uh, he had dirty shoes."

NOT WAITING FOR THE SUN TO RISE

Judith Ann Pelio

There's a dark cloud overhead; escape is impossible.
The beauty of the stars is a shield from the pain.
But the demons come out, and the militia's engaged;
The battle of a constant war feels overwhelming.

The secret atrocities of this war remain unspoken,
For the reality of night is mightier than the façade of day.
The cocoon is a blanket of protection from the sinful truth,
And through the sharpness of the knife, the war goes on.

Dues were paid, in unimaginable ways,
Reflected in the chaos and noise of the night.
Is it a dream this time, or is it happening, again?
The imagination transforms into truth, into this war.

There are no strategies in this persistent battle,
For as sure as the night will be followed by the day,
The enemy will approach, and the struggles prove useless.
This war prevails again, and again, and again!

The eyes become blurred, the throat constricts,
The jaw tightly clenches, and anxiety rapidly soars.
Then, when there is little room at the end of the rope,
The definitive truth is: You Can Only Make a Noose!

TATER

Virginia Smythe

"Oh my Dog! Oh my Dog! She's home, guys! She's HOME!" I bark at the top of my lungs. My barking jostles my brother and sister from their afternoon naps on the couch. I've already had my nap, and taken my position by the door waiting. I am very busy. While those two lazybones slept, I waited. Waited and waited and waited. Very busy.

Monster and Mrs. Wiggles are lazy. How could they sleep knowing mom would come home at any time? Blinking their eyes and shaking off their cat naps, they are caught up in the excitement. *Cat naps? Hmph. Isn't that a funny concept? I mean... We. Are. Dogs. Why on earth is a snooze called a cat nap?*

The frenetic energy of my pack accelerates. *Darn it! Stupid Monster and Mrs. Wiggles. Get out of my way.* We dance with joy by the magic door off of the garage. *I'll just have to bark louder and jump higher than the two of them.*

The door opens. "Mom, Mom, Mom! I missed you so much! I missed you much more than they did. Mom, look at me! Look at me!" I'm doing that thing I do — jumping, running in circles, shrieking, and vying for mom's attention. "Isn't she just the best, guys?" Circle. "I missed her so, so much!" Circle. "She was gone *all* day! That is just way too long." Jump. "Oh my Dog! I missed her!". Circle, circle, jump. "Mom, look at me! I know I missed you the most! Pay attention to ME." I'm doing my best to grab her attention as mom struggles into the house trying not to step on us.

"Ok, ok, guys, *blah blah blah. Blah blah* into the house" giggles Mom. "Let's go outside *blah blah* make puddles. I'm sorry *blah blah* I had to be away so long *blah blah blah* but I had to work to bring home the bacon." I wish Mom could bark because I never understand everything she says. Until Mom learns to bark, I've mastered several of her words. Like, I can totally understand and hear these words and phrases from probably, like a mile away: cookie, chicken, bacon, kisses, bath time, go for a walk, and ride in the car. Oh my Dog! I totally love to go for rides in the car. I don't even care where we are going, I just love being in the car. Some of her words are harder to hear: off, stop, later, bad, and no. I don't like these words one bit. Don't tell Mom, but sometimes, I pretend I can't hear those words, even if she's yelling. Whoops, I'm off topic again. Where was I? Oh yeah…

"Oh my Dog! Did you hear that, guys? Mom said BACON!" I run to the door that goes to the yard. Circle. Wiggles and Monster are on my tail. I'm thinking that if Mom is giving us bacon as our treat today, I want to be the first to run outside, first to do my puddles, and the first in line for bacon. I'm sure I'll be the first. Circle. Circle. Jump!

Finally, Mom reaches the back door and opens it. *Darn it! I wanted to be first out of the door… well, I can still be the first to puddle.* I run to the closest bush. Just as I finish my business with the bush, I see him. *That damn squirrel! What is he doing here?* I speed away after that little nuisance. *Why is he back? Tresspasser! Interloper! I thought I made myself clear yesterday. Damn tree rat! This is MY yard.*

Ah, I feel better now. I'd better check the rest of the yard. I put my nose to the ground and trot along the fence line. Checking the fence — I guess it's kind of our job as dogs. *I mean, Monster and Wiggles do it. And, the dog in the next yard does it too. Do all dogs do it?*

I don't always like having siblings because I don't like to share my Mom. But, when it's time to check the fence, I appreciate having coworkers. It's a big job. Big job, indeed. Big responsibilities. I guess it's nice to have friends to hang out with and, okay, it's kind of cool to have nap buddies. Alright, I guess I really do like my brother and sister. Well, not all of the time, but most of the time.

Besides fence duties, my pack has other jobs. Get this: although it might sound ridiculous, one of Monster's jobs is to bring Mom his toy of the day — sometimes it's his stuffed piggy, sometimes it's his squeaky frog, sometimes it's just one of Joaquin's worn, smelly socks. Anyway, he always insists she throw his toy. What a weirdo! And, like the weirdo he is, he'll run after it, bring it back to her, and then insist she throw it again. And, he'll do this over and over and over again. Mom and Monster call this job "Fetch". I call it B-O-R-I-N-G.

Wiggles' job is much more important than Monster's game of Fetch. *Or so she thinks.* She will often request overtime for yard security. Can you believe it? Overtime. I don't get it. I mean, we've already checked and rechecked the entire perimeter. We've peed on everything. The yard has been patroled, marked, and cleared. But, hey if she feels the need to inspect it more than that, I say, go for it. Personally, I'd rather get on with my other important duty of sitting on Mom's lap to keep her company. Oh, I almost forgot, Wiggles also has a job of sitting under the little palm tree, practicing meditation and studying birds. Me? I'm more of a ground guy - squirrels, lizards, frogs, and toads. But, don't get me started on those toads. Those jerks have sent me to the emergency room a few times! *Damn poisonous toads!*

So, a little bit more about *moi*: Tate is the name. Melting hearts is my game. You can call me Tate, Tater, or by my formal name — Little Man Tate. My mom has several nicknames for me, Monster, and Wiggles, but those are personal.

A couple of important facts: I want to clear this one up right away — I am adopted. Mom has always been forthcoming about this as she doesn't like to keep secrets from me. Also, I believe in a higher Dog. How else could I have come to live with such a great adoptive Mom? She's always got a warm lap, a gentle, petting nature, and kind words for me. Kind words, well, most of the time, unless I'm bad. And we are not going to talk about that.

I don't remember much about my birth mother, but I think I come from a place called Yorkshire and, I am of Terrier descent. We are a proud and stubborn tribe. This has to be true because I do what I want and when I want. I am four and half pounds, and, quite frankly, adorable, with a face that melts most peoples' hearts.

I'm not modest or shy. Mom says I am strong-willed. Again, don't tell me what to do — I do what I want, when I want. Rules. Schmules. I think they must have made rules for labradors, beagles, and poodles, not for handsome, lizard-chasing, lap-loving, treat hustlers like me.

Mom put up baby gates to keep me and my siblings confined to the great room and kitchen area. But, that gate doesn't stop me. No sireee! Before I learned how to open the gate, I simply slipped through the slats in the gate. Being a little larger than pocket-size, allows me to not only slip through these forbidden zones; but, I go more places than my brother Monster, who is a lanky 6 pounds., and far more places than big ol' Mrs. Wiggles who tops the scales at over 10 pounds. I consider myself a lover and a fighter. Just ask the wildlife in my yard — I really put the fear of Dog in them. But the other side of me is sweet, gentle, and loving. You can ask my Mom, she'll tell you. Wait! Is that Mom talking?

"Cookies!" trills Mom.

"OH MY DOG! I gotta go. It's cookie time!"

BOBBY AND HIS SLINGSHOT

Jim Wiggins

Bobby lived on a farm with his parents and an older brother, Ray. He was jealous of his brother because Ray owned a 12 gauge shotgun that Bobby wasn't allowed to touch. Sometimes his brother brought home squirrels or rabbits to eat and was greeted like a hero by his parents.

Bobby decided to make himself a slingshot. All he needed were two wide rubber bands cut from an old inner tube and a v-shaped handle that was easily cut from guava or china berry trees. Each rubber band was affixed to the tips of the handle with string tied real strong to avoid slipping. The leather tongue from an old shoe was attached in the center of the rubber bands by punching holes with an ice pick to provide a pocket for the ammunition (usually small rocks).

Bobby was quite proud of his sling shot and couldn't wait to try it out. He practiced shooting tin cans placed at a distance and got better each day at hitting his target. Still, Ray kept bringing in game from time to time to time and seemed to enjoy killing things.

One day Bobby surprised a covey of quail in one of the hedgerows and instinctively pulled out his slingshot when they flew. He shot blindly as they scattered in the air.

Afterwards, he heard a noise in the hedgerow. A quail was thrashing about and seemed unable to fly. Bobby moved closer and gently picked it up. He stroked its head as the eyes looked into his as if to say," Help Me."

Bobby touched his lip to its beak and tried to blow some air into its lungs, but to no avail. He whispered, ''I'm sorry" and walked away.

When he got home he went into his bedroom and put the slingshot on the top shelf in his closet. He was never jealous of his brother again and realized that guns and slingshots were made for the sole purpose of killing

FALSE LOVE

Richard Paul Angelini

What took her away?
Chance?
Hope?
Risk?
Time?
The old stain of beauty
Her guard against rhyme?

Love's message needs
Understanding,
Rhythm,
Rhyme,
Meter.
Yet her smile forsakes all.
The face of a deceiver.

"It once was and now is not,"
Her easy lie does conceal.
Truth is lost
Never to reveal,
Jewels of a false love once clothed my soul.

PHILIPPINE ADVENTURE

Margie Bonner

The beginning:

When I decided to write this account as a memoir, I did not realize just how difficult it would be. To make it accurate, my memory had to go back over 55 years.

The year was 1962. The Pam American plane was huge. The drone of its engines was soothing. I had never been on a plane before yet strangely, I was relaxed. Cindy, my two year old daughter, slept soundly beside me, her head in my lap. We had boarded the plane at Travis Air Base in California. I remember struggling to climb the stairs while carrying a sleeping child. We were now on our way, facing a 14 hour flight to Clark Air Force Base, in the Philippine Islands, which was our final destination.

It had been five months since the family had been together. My husband had to go first to report to his new assignment and to obtain military approved housing for us, his dependents. Once he had left, I truly felt alone and lost. I had obtained my driver's license while he was with me. Much to my embarrassment, I failed the driving portion twice but managed to obtain it on the third try. I felt the examiner gave me the okay due to the tears shining in my eyes.

Once my husband was gone, I was now in charge. The entire process took many trips to the base. When travelling to a tropical foreign country, immunizations were required to protect our health. Cindy was very mature for her age. I clearly explained the process, always stressing the underlining reason for the many bi-weekly injections. “This was the only way we could go and see Daddy” I said. She marched into the clinic like a little soldier. Holding up her arm with never a tear, if she could be strong, so could I.

Cindy is now stirring beside me. Waking up and looking about, her big brown eyes full of excitement and curiosity, saying the words all parents are familiar with.

‘’Are we there yet”?

Hours were ahead of us. We eat, play games, look out the window, and try to imagine what shapes the clouds are forming. Thankfully, we both take plenty of naps, and all in all the hours pass.

The pilot has informed us we would be landing in the next hour. There is a buzz within the plane. Passengers are gathering up belongings, chattering to one another. A sense of excitement fills the air. I had taken Cindy to the bathroom earlier. Washing her face, combing her hair, changing her clothes, this was important to me. We had to look our best. I also had chosen a new dress. Thinking back I wonder why I had chosen that particular outfit: black dress, very fitted, with a white collar, black shoes with small stacked heels completed the outfit. Dear God, what was I thinking when I bought the outfit? I was not going for a job interview, yet somehow I felt the dress portrayed a woman in control, perhaps to cover up how unsure I really was. Stepping into a new world was daunting, and I was totally unprepared. I never remember wearing the dress again.

Stepping off the plane, Cindy's hand clutched tightly, I took a moment to look about the airfield. The sky was a deep blue, the air that brushed my cheeks was warm, much the California air that we had just left. A mass of people were waiting for their loved ones to appear. The men looking eagerly toward the door were all in Air Force Blue, hard to distinguish one from another. Holding tight to Cindy's hand, we made our first steps downward. Finally, I spotted my husband, who had taken his hat off and was waving it frantically. Cindy began to squeal in delight:

"Daddy, Daddy!" I felt her hand slip from mine as she ran into the waiting arms of her father. I also ran toward my husband. He was holding Cindy, her face snuggled into his neck. I felt his arms engulf me the familiar smell of his uniform was a relief and a comfort.

We were safe, and we were home. The Philippine Adventure had just begun.

WHEN DIVORCE IS A GOOD THING!

Karina G. Felix

The Constant Nagger.

Even thought the male likes to make the female counterpart, the naggers in a relationship, in actuality the male that is the constant complainer. The male will find that one moment or time to keep harping that everything was your fault because of that one incident. We know they use it as the only ammunition they can find, because they can't find something better to play the blame-game.

The Non-listener.

The female expresses her feelings with words. The male doesn't listen. We wonder why issues are not being resolved. The answer is very simple. Not until it's too late and the breaking point has arrived, then only will they claim: "But you should have told me this before".

He has a house. You have a home.

The male sees a house as real estate. What's the value now and what will the value be upon selling the property. The female takes that house and convert it into a home; a place where they can invite family and friend, and one day raise their children with family traditions and new customs. When the male stops paying attention to the home, he pretty much stops paying attention to the family and marriage. The home is an extension of the marriage.

Your mirror is looking back

You look into the mirror and you wonder: whom that person is staring back at you? You can't remember when the original person that occupied that body left, and left you behind with a stranger. You finally, realize that you have been lost and now the road to finding yourself once more becomes a hard and long return to reality

The world is lifted off your shoulder.

He walks out the door and you feel the weight of the world just totally lifted off of your shoulders. You can breathe, jump and laugh again. You find and recognize your old self and you can't believe you've lived that long without your true self.

WILD ANGELS

Virginia Guido

As a child, I believed Christmas was magical, an occasion filled with smiling people, brightly-wrapped gifts, and jingling bells. By the time I was six years old, my mother changed my idea of Christmas forever. It took her less than two hours to achieve that.

One evening, early in December, Mom came home from work to find my two older sisters and I had already put up our artificial Christmas tree. There wasn't much exertion involved in this endeavor. The tree was a spindly imitation of pine needles stuck in a weighted block resembling a toy soldier's drum.

Mom pursed her lips. We weren't sure if our little venture had her approval but we did expect some praise for not breaking any ornaments. Nope. Mom did not give out commendations for following her instructions. She repositioned some of the decorations, attractive ones in the front, not so pretty types in the back. Ironically, the tree itself was not appealing, no matter where you placed anything.

We all laughed, including Mom, while throwing strands of silver tinsel over the tree, hoping to mask the shabby branches. The scene could have been a Norman Rockwell painting, minus the presence of a father figure. Just as we were about to step back and admire our effort, mom dug deep into her large pocketbook.

"Look what I bought today," she said as she produced a cellophane bag of white-cotton candy. "Some man came into the office selling this. He called it Angel Hair".

It was not white-cotton candy, but it sure looked like white-cotton candy. We were wide-eyed and hoping to smell the cloying scent of spun sugar as she opened the package. Instead she began separating the thin white fibers. Mom gave some to each of us to toss on the tree. We followed her lead: separating it, tossing it, and gently letting it drift down to whatever frail branches caught their descent. This was even more fun and nicer looking than the tinsel. The fun and enjoyment was short-lived.

My oldest sister started scratching her arms through her sweater, and we noticed red bumps appearing all over her pale skin. Then my mother started to sneeze; her eyes became red and her face blotchy. Finally, my older sister and I were coughing, almost to the point of gagging, without reprieve. What was in this angel hair? None of us were willing to remove the offensive product from our pathetic tree. Yet, we couldn't keep this Christmas catastrophe in the house either.

"Quick, open the kitchen window!" my mother bellowed with the finesse of a drill sergeant.

My oldest sister struggled to open the window, which was frozen shut due to the three inches of snow on the ledge. Mom picked up the tree, tinsel, ornaments, and all, carried it to the kitchen, and hoisted it out that open window onto the empty lot behind our house.

For the rest of the month, I would look out the window at

our forlorn, dejected, and sad tree. Would we still have Christmas? Should we go to church and apologize to Baby Jesus for stealing the hair of His angels? Is Santa going to be mad and not bring us presents? One thing was for sure; this would be a Christmas without a Christmas tree. In a matter of 120 minutes, we went from a Norman Rockwell Christmas to a Norman Bates Holiday.

By January, the city workers had carted the tree away — along with other debris. But that year we still received gifts, made family visits, sang carols, and shared in fun and laughter.

Our Yuletide wasn't ruined after all. That angel hair incident taught me the season is defined by how we feel in our hearts as a family, how blessed we really are, and not what we put up for show. To this day, I hold on to that sentiment each and every year, for my children and my grandchildren.

My name is Virginia and, yes, I do believe in the spirit of Christmas.

SKIPPING STONES

Donna S. Fernandez

My friend and I sit by
the canal's edge and remember
smiles
frowns
friends
here and there
or gone
in some cases.

We speak of fresh paths
treaded alone oftentimes
and wonder
what we'd each think
of those disparate journeys.

Stones skip personal
ebbs
flows
tides.
A step, slide, step
of a syncopated waltz
time kept by laughs
and some tears.

We went separate ways
we confessed.
But the triumphant find,
while skipping stones
in this green and sunlit place
Is that
we are
and still remain
the best of friends.

A NEW FRIEND

Jim Wiggins

The irrigation ditches were filled with water flowing through the cane field. Amni sat cross-legged as he watched a floating twig swish by. Then he uncrossed his legs and dangled his feet in the cool water.

Oh, that feels so good, he thought. It's so hot today.

Nearby, his muscular sweaty father used a machete to whack away the tasseled stalks of cane and tossed them on the wagon, which waited to haul the stalks to the warehouse. Amni knew they would be crushed by big machines, and the sweet juice would eventually be turned into sugar. The black men around his father did the same, cutting a wide swath of cane.

Suddenly, Amni heard a different sound. There was something moving through the cane. It was moving in his direction. Could it be a wild animal? His heart was in his throat. He was getting ready to run when he was surprised by a white boy about his age who stepped through the stalks of the cane and into the clearing.

"Hello there. I'm sorry if I startled you. I didn't mean to scare you. My name is Stan. I live in the big house at the other side of the quarters."

"Yes, you scare me. But now I no scared. I know who you are. My name, Amni."

Stan sat down near Amni at the edge of the ditch and put his feet in the water, too. "Boy, it's a hot day! This sure feels good."

Amni didn't know what to say. After all, he had never been around white children very much. Slave children were taught to "keep their place." Few were able to read or write, nor did they have many of the privileges that the white man enjoyed. Their homes were clapboard shacks that had no heat or plumbing, making their lives were very different.

After a few minutes of awkward silence, Stan asked, "Are you a slave?" He hoped that Amni would understand. Amni thought about it for a few moments and finally stammered, "Yes. Yes. I slave. My father slave, my mother slave. My brother, sister, slave. Ever'body slave. Amni pointed in the direction of his father who was working nearby and proudly said, "That my father. He work from early morning 'til the sun goes down. He and other slaves cut much cane."

Stan nodded in the direction of a tall white man who sat tall and straight in the saddle on a horse and said, "That is my father. He is an overseer." Stan's father held the reins of the horse in one hand and a whip in the other.

After a few moments, Stan asked Amni if he would like to race boats. Amni didn't understand. He gasped when Stan pulled a knife out from his pocket and began to whittle on two small sticks. He carved them in the shape of two tiny boats, and after a few minutes handed one to Amni. Then they lined up the boats next to each other in the swift water and let them go.

The boats shot quickly through the water as each boy hovered nearby and followed the boats for a long distance through the cane field until they came to rest side by side, snagged by a rock. No one was the winner. But they both felt like winners.

Each of them had found a new friend.

A CHEF'S PRAYER

Hartley Barnes

When I leave this world and return to it, or another one, let me be a chef.

Allow me to take nature's gifts and create experiences for the palate. Let my hands invent with spices and herbs, adventures to titillate body and soul. Give me the ability to concoct ideas to stimulate mind and flesh that leads to joyful orgasms.

Let me think outside the box while listening to the rhythms of pots and pans. Formulate flavors that dance in the mouth; produce nuances, with John Coltrane's saxophone in the background. Endow me with ideas not yet discovered to provoke love without inhibitions.

Fill me with secrets that will materialize on tables to satisfy the most discriminating and instigate suggestive conversations. I want to bake with sweet sugars, exuding aromas that permeate spaces with desires to explore. Let me be a magician with sustenance to unleash our most inner thoughts, freeing ourselves to take chances with each other.

Give me the aptitude to develop that which will arouse passion and sing to the senses in four-part harmony. Along with wines and salutations, enable my creations to entertain the intellect with mysteries and sensations to awaken the subconscious.

Free the wildness in me with subtleties to fill the inner

being with ecstasy and placate the receiver with each spoon of—what is this?

IF I COULD SAY

Richard Paul Angelini

If I could say...
You the visible mystery
The conquering femininity
Do magically remove all misery
And I, in wonder waiting...

If I could say...
Passionate kissings of the night
Smother all fears until light
Releasing dreams of their bite
And I, all misunderstanding...

If I could say...
My definitive truth not uttered
For fear of shallow thoughts muttered
Yet, our hearts together fluttered
In our place of rest...

If I could say...
My dearest wished affect
Would cause your heart to reflect
On years and decades of un-rechecked
Love...

Then I could say.

HELLO, HELLO

Don Conway

Hello, hello? Earth can you hear me? This is God calling. Yes, that God. I thought it was time we had a talk.

I'm calling to tell you that I am really pissed off at all, well, almost all, of you.

Look, I gave you this lovely planet and what have you done with it: you've polluted the air, cut down acres and acres of trees, filled most of its rivers with toxic runoffs. And now your f_ _ _ _ing up the oceans with tons and tons of plastic garbage.

I put lots of beautiful animals down there for you to share the earth with and you are driving them into extinction faster than I can create them. Whales, elephants, polar bears...you are killing them off as if you hated them. That was not the plan.

I gave you Beethoven, Einstein, Rembrandt, Da Vinci, Shakespeare and Winston Churchill to occupy your minds and you developed Punk Rock and Donald Trump! Is that really the best you can do?

Listen Earth, it's been a while since I've done anything really radical but I still know how to cause a flood if I choose to. And this time there will be no Noah — so don't make me come down there.

Shape-up Earth or it will really be goodbye for you.

I will not call you a second time.

Goodbye.

THE SEARCH PARTY

Virginia Smythe

Before the pageantry of the ceremony began,
I held you tightly in the palm of my hand.
Joy, with you, I was truly entwined.
I yearn for my yesterdays when I was naive and blind.

You were always near, a true and close friend.
I selfishly assumed you'd be mine until the end.
Responsibility, maturity, and marriage came knocking.
You became distant. I began sleepwalking.

Days fade to months and months to years.
You abandoned me to deal with my tears.
Was your departure punishment for our failure?
Or circumstantial being there with my jailor?

A band of gold was no reason to leave.
It was the memory of you for which I grieved.
The deteriorating wedding party of two,
Could have used a strong dosage of you.

Marital destiny became cantankerous reality.
We said goodbye to Lightheartedness and Joviality.
Misery came for a visit and joined our mechanical dance.
No more laughter, romance, or holding hands.

Gray, dim days turned to total eclipse.
Nobody warned us or gave us a script.
We sat together, but alone, feeling blue,
Realizing Hope and Serenity took vacation, too.

Discontent and Apathy became the new norm.
Oh, Joy, it was for you that we mourned.
Misery, once just a visitor, became the permanent guest.
No longer did our new and fragile union feel blessed.

Melancholy and Sadness
Invited Frustration and Madness.
Anger crashed the party and proposed to Despair.
Nothing made sense — it didn't seem fair.

Desire and Trust choked on the lies,
The twosome continued to cohabitate in disguise.
'Fake it until you make it' was the internal mantra,
Phony fondness for each other the outward propaganda.

Resentment invited Bitterness to the gloomy reception.
Thank the heavens above there was never conception.
The soiree of Love once seemed unwavering and strong,
Was simply an illusion — an infatuation gone wrong.

Anxiety and Discomfort took root on the stage,
Leaving the couple full of Hostility and Rage.
Happiness and Bliss could barely be heard,
Once the cesspool of disagreement was violently stirred.

The noise and confusion that sweept through the bash,
Exposed a strong indication of the marital clash.
The helpless duo no longer belonged,
To the feeling portrayed in their ethereal love song.

Appetizers of lawyers, papers, and court dates were served.
The announcement left friends and family unnerved.
Property was divided before the second course.
Mr. and Mrs. titles swiftly changed by divorce.

The after-party included an encounter with Grief and Depression.
The rediscovery of you, Joy, became my obsession.
But before the search party could commence,
Anger and Mourning stopped by for one last dance.

Are you a dream or flashback of a life that came before?
Tell me. Was it me who pushed you out the door?
Joy, come back to my heart where you belong
Do not declare youth our swan song.

Name changed back to the maiden,
A significant step — I was feeling so brazen.
Time did pass and the wounds did heal,
So grateful to be off that hamster wheel.

Once I realized Joy was a conscious decision,
My mind was one tracked — I had tunnel vision.
I used to blame him for your exodus.
Perhaps the ‘we’ should never have been an ‘us’.

My rearview mirror vision becomes clearer,
As I feel you getting nearer and nearer.
It is your homecoming for which I await,
The feeling of you is my favorite trait.

Now raise your glass for the couple's final toast,
Their contract of marriage is now just a ghost.
Say goodbye to the Guilt and Shame of the past,
Joy has reappeared in the spotlight — at last!

Matrimonious traditions absolutely endure.
But I am Content being out of that manure.
Joy, you are the one that I will continually chase,
So Happy to be away from that dark, negative space.

I may sound aloof, harsh and sarcastic,
But I can no longer pretend or perform being plastic.
Now… true to myself — never compromising on less,
It is Joy I embrace — I choose to fluoresce.

The next party I give, or celebration I attend,
Joy will be my companion, but not my only friend.
I'll invite Laughter, Levity, and Cheer,
If you want to come along, you can bring the beer.

A CHAPTER IN MY LIFE

Gloria H. Ferrara

Brooklyn, New York. P.S. 123

From first grade, six years old, walking with my older sister Mary, each day was routine, until I reached fourth grade. In seventh grade she was the Flag monitor. Duties were to place a white flag from an open window shouting school had begun.

During lunch/recess, this continued, flag in, school open, flag out. School day over at 3:00. "You know Flags in Flags out, she is my big sister" I announced with pride to my school friends. It was a very important thing my sister did.

Classes consisted of boys and girls, until the boys continued in rooms at the upper level of the school building.

J.H.S. P.S. 162

An all-girl school a few blocks further. English class consisted of grammar, home making, included cooking. I enjoyed that class. On certain days, classes were alternating between cooking, which emphasized keeping our work area clean and shiny, (stove, counter, pots, and pans.) And the next day cooking lessons consisted learning how to use measuring cups, heating an oven, and preparing a meal, with entree, salad, and desert. We loved eating the meals we cooked.

In a room equiped with beds, we were taught how to make a bed; tucking the flat sheet at the corners. I still use this system. The class which was special for me was drawing. We learned how to draw the human figure and face. My classmate drew my face, and I, in turn, drew Pauline. I was pleased to see the drawing of my face was chosen to be placed on a wall. My drawing of Pauline was not featured, but I kept it with a collection pencil drawing in a special scrap book.

Sewing class entailed learning how to use a sewing machine, and once we were proficient, we were assigned to sew our gym wear. I must say, we did a splendid job, and were able to wear what we made to all our gym class. Our sewing teacher was sure to remind us that she was a personal friend of the famous Edith Head who clothed many movie stars, such as Audrey Hepburn.

Another teacher Miss Hans taught us clay pottery. When we graduated, we were expected, and truly thought we were ready for the next step in learning.

William H. Maxwell High School

William H. Maxwell had taken over the school, formally known as East New York High, an all- girl school. Courses offered were: Beauty Culture, and Secretarial. Riding the subway from my home in Brooklyn, at Jefferson Station, exchanged to an elevated trains line at Eastern Parkway. All students were given special passes to ride the El free. During my senior year, I have a boyfriend. He drives a beautiful blue and white car. Watching from window girls lined up to see if they had a ride and if a boy was waiting. Most days when he could take off from his work, he came.

My curriculum was Stenography, taking dictation, transcribing and typing it. Stenography class, leaning to use a mimeograph copy machine, transcribing short hand to letters, making carbon copies of them, to use the adding machine, without looking, just as we did while transcribing our shorthand.

MOTHER NATURE

D.M. Littlefield

I'm trying to write about colors without naming them, but my muse won't cooperate, so my mind starts wandering. I glance at my watch and think about time. I wonder how time became known as Father Time, winter as Old Man Winter, and nature as Mother Nature.

I believe the natural world is named Mother Nature because she's similar to a woman who is tired from raising a large family. She is exhausted after the long growing season, so in late fall, Father Time orders her to rest. Her friend, Old Man Winter, assures her that he will take care of things. He puts everything to sleep and covers it with a soft fluffy blanket of snow. Months pass while Mother Nature rests and regains her strength.

In spring, she feels energized again, and as any woman would, decides to make herself presentable. She has the strong March winds comb the dead branches out of the trees and pile the faded fallen leaves in neat mounds next to fences. She sends April showers to splash awake all the sleeping trees, bushes, plants, and grass. Then she chooses the brightest colors of finery from her vast wardrobe. She dresses herself in varied flowers—daffodils, tulips, forsythias, wisterias, irises, and many shades of azaleas. Then she adds the beautiful colors of cherry, pear, peach, and apple blossoms. For the final touch, she adds the fragrances of hyacinths, lilacs, and honeysuckle.

I didn't mention any colors, but I hope you saw them as I did.

JUST ADJUST!

Karina. G. Felix

I have been searching for peace, quiet and serenity. When I couldn't find it, I focused on reading, listening to music and meditation.

I found some of it, but I was still looking for a deeper feeling of peace within my mind and heart. And so believed that by transforming my home, I'd find it there.

I arranged and rearranged the house. Switching furniture's locations. Replacing paintings on the wall. Adding cozy lighting, candles and night-lights.

I immersed in studies on Reiki and Chakra Healing. I've introduced aromatherapy, crystals, smudging and chanting with good intentions into the home. I brought the noise level down in search of Zen.

I created an outdoor oasis in my back yard with night blooming Jasmines, Gardenias, my prized avocados, mangos, bananas, lemon trees and more. I've created the routines to make each and every single space feel and mean something.

I am happy in my environment. My home is warm and cozy. Everyone enjoys visiting and hanging around. There is a calm and relaxing feeling the minute you walk in. The orange lights of the salt rocks and the scents of essence oils wafting through the A/C system.

I've created my oasis, but where is my peace and serenity. I've arranged the home, but where is the quiet. I chant my appreciation for my abundance of the beautiful flowers and fruits in my yard. Yet, I can't find the inner peace I've been searching for.

And then it finally sunk in…. I have diligently made the right changes and adjustments in my outer world, but totally neglected to channel that same energy into my inner being. Once analyzed, I found the missing part of that 'Peace'.

My outlook in life was a bit distorted. I had to find a way to accept life as it is. As we see it in our own reality mind and then find a way to adjust to that illusion.

Each and every morning, we get to wake up and decide the outcome of our day. We get to take back control of our life; how we feel about what is happening in our lives and how we choose to re-act to those curve balls that life throws at us.

Who we see and how we choose to accept what is said, whether it goes with our beliefs or not. Just smile, take a deep breath, let it out slowly and allow yourself to just be.

It's not your issue, but you do get to decide whether you will participate or not. The bottom line is, you have a choice to decide how you will feel right here, right now… and adjust.

When the days become too much to handle, make a conscious effort, take a step back and assess the situation. Remind yourself that reality is only as you perceive it and everything else is an illusion until you give it a path.

Choose to take responsibility for all your actions. Empower yourself to be in control of your life, your decisions, your destination, your journey and your freedom. Consciously choose your way of accepting all that has happened, is happening and will happen in your life.

Look at each situation individually, analyze the pros and cons, and all the life lessons that comes with it, and never again feel lost, alone, doubtful, fearful and uncertain.

This conscious state-of-being allows you to manifest your desires freely, and expeditiously. Our life is an illusion. It is our perceived understanding of what we believe to be true.

In this conscious state-of-being you can genuinely live life fully in abundance, appreciation, acceptance and happiness.

So, just adjust!

PHILIPPINE ADVENTURE II

Margie Bonner

Our First Home

Weeks passed in a blur. My husband had rented a cement block house in the town of Angeles, Province of Pampanga. The house was simple in construction, with an open floor plan. Two sets of windows faced the street. The front door had a large window and a nice snug screen door. This appealed to me as I loved a natural breeze. It could have been a house located in any town in America. The one thing that I pondered was the block fence around the house, with rolls of barbed wire imbedded on the top. Why? I wondered. Was there hidden danger I knew nothing about?

The house was located in the middle of the homes lived in by the citizens of the town. The narrow streets were not paved but were worn smooth with shell rock formed from years of use. Cindy and I spent a lot of time sitting on the front step with the gate opened trying to observe all we could see and hear. I have since learned that the Philippines is made up of over seven thousand islands with 175 languages spoken. The main languages were Tagalong and Filipino. The sounds and smells were fascinating. We were both eager to embrace our new homeland.

In renting the house, my husband also arranged a guard and a maid. I am sure it was all with the recommendation of his fellow GI's. The maid he had hired was young, with a sweet, eager face.

She spoke some English, but she appeared to understand everything I said. The guard, I never saw. His job was to keep an eye on the house, especially from 4am to 8am. These were the critical hours my husband was most concerned about. Despite his precautions, our home was robbed about 10 days after our arrival. That morning I walked out into the main part of the house, and I felt something amiss. We had very little in the home but what could be picked up and removed was gone. This included a radio, a guitar, and other odds and ends. When my husband arrived home and was told what had occurred, he was furious. Marching down the street to find the guard, he no doubt vented his feelings. I left the entire episode alone; the feelings of violation not forgotten, we carried on.

Getting used to a maid in the house was not difficult. She was quiet and very efficient. One incident I remember clearly. She was in the bedroom making up the bed. Later I saw she had stripped all the linens from the bed and shoved the mattress close to the wall. The linen was folded carefully and placed at the foot of the bed. This puzzled me, but I did not say anything. Later I found out the Philippine people slept on mats which they rolled up every morning. I really admired her ingenuity to try and solve an issue she knew nothing about. The next morning I showed her how to make the bed. She gave me a smile in complete understanding.

The house did not have a washing machine. This was actually the norm. A cement slab with a hand operated pump and a large metal wash tub underneath was located in the back yard. The entire laundry operation was common, and I soon got used to seeing her, squatting beside the tub with her hands in soapy water with Cindy at her side. Cindy was talking non-stop, smiles and nods on the maid's face. What a true awakening I was having, with me being the one who was sure we did not need a maid.

The street was busy with traffic. The main form of transportation was jitneys and a single horse drawn carriage known as a celesa. The jitneys were decorated in a design that was pleasing to their owners. They were beautiful with a lot of floral decorations. Riding in the celesta was Cindy's and my favorite mode. We loved sitting high up on the bench seat behind the driver and horse on our way to the open air market. We did this with no fear within only a month of our arrival. The people we met were so friendly all with wide smiles; everyone was drawn to Cindy. Amazingly, she jabbered away and they all seemed to understand her.

I did not know what further adventures would follow but I definitely was enjoying the journey. We stayed in this house for about four or five months, before moving on to a sub-division full of American families. It was with pangs of sadness that we left the tiny block house as it had sheltered my family and had welcomed us. I know I would miss the busy street and the closeness of the town. More adventures awaited.

IN PASSING YEARS

Richard Paul Angelini

"If I could have a thousand years--just one
little thousand years--more of life, I might,
in that time, draw near enough to true
Romance to touch the hem of her robe."
O'Henry

Time passes sweetly through
Thoughts of what was,
Now is,
And will be tomorrow.

By the park bench her young love stood
Waiting,
Wanting,
Unknowing,
Unseen.

She, drowned in innocent confusion,
Sweet unknown, folding into night.
Love not un-welcome, passes quickly by.
Her true hopes felt, still unspoken.

Tomorrows rush changes.
Like a wrinkled ripe promise his heart still lingers,

Still wanting.

She has returned.
Her fragrant body now like spring leaves browned with autumn's approach.
Yet the memory of bright fruit is pressed upon her skin.
She carries a hope for him.

His rescue, a fallen rose from her soft hand is returned to her grasp.
Eyes unite,
Breaths deepen,
Un-expecting lips find the kiss.
But who can say which?
It is to be.

PEARL HARBOR INCIDENT ON NIIHAUA ISLAND

Jim Wiggins

Sigeroi Nikisfikalchi was a Japanese pilot who crash landed on the island of Niihau after bombing Pearl Harbor.

His "ZERO" plane went through the Okoli Pass, circled over Wakiawa on the island of Oahu.

Then he and his plane went down in the countryside of the small isolated island near a sugar cane field.

It is said that the locals were so infuriated that they dragged him out of the wreckage and killed him with the use of machetes and stones.

The pilot from Japan certainly didn't expect that change of events.

Serves him right.

SILENT SOUND

Donna S. Fernandez

Sound that no sound makes is solitary.

Sound that no sound makes is collective.

Sounds of no sound can be
the solitary gathering of
exhaled breaths of
    an ant
    a ladybug, or
    a hummingbird.

And can sound without sound
gather in unison with sound
    as when moving air
    fingers the harp of Aspen leaves ?
    or the sonorous trails of an owl's hoot?

Just what is sound in the absence of sound?
Who has heard the sound that no sound can make?
Can I hear what cannot be heard?

And who is there to measure or plot
    sound without sound
        this sound that no sound can make?
This silent sound.

FREE SPEECH

Hartley Barnes

Free speech— is it free?

What is your stance for those who stand, sit, kneel, or turn their backs to what is paying homage to the country?

According to the First Amendment in the United States Constitution, an individual has the right to express his or her opinion without fear of retribution from the government, but not from his or her neighbors, friends, or adversaries. As long as the well-being of our fellow citizens is not jeopardized, falsely accused or threatened with corporal harm, we are free to speak out. We will not always agree for many reasons. We do not think alike (we are not clones), but likewise. Rejoinders to one's opinion usually come from personal feelings, upbringing, exposure, respect and no respect for opinions. What is free speech?

A ballplayer kneels during the playing of the national anthem. Who is he jeopardizing? Who is he falsely accusing? Who is he threatening? Does he not have a right to protest and not be denounced for doing so? Many of those who oppose will say these ballplayers are rich and privileged. Why are they disrespecting the anthem and flag? Making money does not negate one's right to opposition. Their talents that generate money, and lots of it, are not an excuse to remain silent, over social issues that are dissecting our country. Others will simply react because they are chauvinistic. The flag is a symbol representing, supposedly, a free country. It is not God. If we are truly at liberty, where is the veneration for our sentiments?

Individuals are singled out, for their opposing views, and are characterized as having an attitude. It is not a secret; we all have attitudes, and so, there is no foundation to stand on when using that label. It is another way to say someone is a rabble-rouser and unpatriotic. Disagreements are based on many facts: ignorance, intolerance, false sense of superiority. Ethnicity, socioeconomic standing, the color of skin, religious persuasion, etc. dictate how responses in many cases formulate. Freedom is costly; it brings out both the superlative and the foulness in us. It can separate not only individuals, but also, groups, races, communities, and the nation. If we are true believers in democracy, where is the reverence for our thoughts?

Equate free speech to fantasy; it is unachievable and unrealistic because of people against people. It does not matter how logical your conversation is, someone is going to find fault with it. Free speech, in its purest sense is in a vicious cycle and will remain that way for perpetuity. The solution to free speech is— free speech!

We must, without malice, conquer our fear of hearing the words of others. Be cognizant. Free speech is not free; it comes with risk. You are open to ridicule: odium, agitator, the bad guy, and a host of other adjectives. Free expression has boundaries; if not, there will be anarchy. It is an oxymoron and requires strength to stand up even against the odds. How strong is your faith with an abstract system? Why should anyone who speaks for or against sensitive subjects become targets for disparagement? It is a complex issue, and as time changes, so will conclusions repeatedly in an attempt to satisfy the opposition. It does not make sense to walk up an escalator that is going down. We must find level ground to stand on with room to pass each other without cynicism. Debate without objectivity is ascending the escalator going down. How does a modern society advertise free speech when, in fact, it is not free?

THE VIOLIN MAKER

Don Conway

*The theme from Fritz Lang's 1927 movie Masterpiece *METROPOLIS*

Time to start another one. Let me see…this will be number…um…279. My how time goes by. The family has been fortunate and we seem to be in some demand. I can only hope that number 279 will live up to our reputation.

He entered the drying room where the treated woods were cured after the harsh chemical soakings. *Maple to start with for the back and ribs. Maple again for the neck but not just yet.* With a keen eye, years of experience, and a certain sense of excitement that always overcame him with the start of a new endeavor, he sifted through the stacks of treated maple wood. It took him an hour to find a particularly handsome piece. *Yes, he thought, this looks very promising. Very promising indeed.* How could he explain to anyone the sense of "rightness" that overcame him when he looked at, weighed, and rubbed his hand over a piece of wood? No explanation was possible. He just "knew" this was the correct wood for this new one.

He carried the piece of maple into his workroom and stood by the window to examine it again in the daylight. For thirty minutes, he looked at it from every angle as he appraised the grain and the flatness. He looked carefully for minute cracks and burrs in the grain. There were none. "Yes, very promising indeed," he murmured.

Satisfied that he had found the correct foundation piece for this new item, he ceased work and spent the rest of the day going over the next steps in his mind. As he mentally reviewed the work, he found several points at which he felt he could make some improvements. He determined to put them into practice.

The week that followed consisted of tracing the bottom shape on the piece of maple, cutting it out and sanding, sanding and more sanding. He found one section of the wood that was thicker than he wanted so that needed sanding again. During the course of that week, a premonition took possession of his mind. *There is something special about this project* he thought with rising excitement. Again, it was beyond explanation, but he knew that "something special" was happening.

Because of this "something special" feeling, he decided to make a fresh pot of glue just for 279. Mixing and boiling the glue took four days. He did it in the family's traditional way and worked slowly to get the consistency just right. In the end, he was satisfied and set the glue pot aside so that no one else in the workroom would use it.

Crafting the ribs was next. He cut them out of the same piece of maple he'd used for the bottom. It was tedious work since there were so many ribs and no two were exactly alike. Each rib was cut, sanded and fitted into its exact place on the bottom piece. It took him eight days to make them and glue them in place but in the end, he was satisfied. *Definitely something special happening here.* He did not mention it to the rest of the family.

The next several steps took him back to the wood drying room; this time for Willow wood. Willow wood is very delicate and because of the "special nature" of this instrument he spent three days just looking for the right pieces of it— eventually, he found them. They were as graceful as a swan's neck but tight grained and light as feathers. After more shaping and sanding, sanding, and sanding he glued them to the ribs.

The top was, of course, the crucial piece. Again, his instinct, his heart, told him that this project called for, and could sustain, something special. Spruce was the wood for the top but here he tried something daring. Several pieces of spruce wood in the drying room were from Croatia but the family had never used it on any of its products. Nevertheless, he decided to use it for 279. Once he found the piece he wanted he spent two days just feeling it, knocking on it to listen for its resonance, and convincing himself that this was the right thing to do. And it was. As he applied the newly mixed varnish (made of gum Arabic, honey and egg whites) the entire piece seemed to meld itself into a single wooden structure. Now he was sure it was special.

The final steps of adding the neck, the tuning pegs, and the bridge took another week. At last, it was ready. He added strings, tuned it, picked up a bow and played a few scales.

Yes, this one is special! Extraordinarily so. It might even prove to be the best one so far he thought as he applied his label to the inside of the body and read: Antonio Stradivari, Cremona, Italy 1723.

TIME IS OURS

Richard Paul Angelini

Come softly this night.
Come into my arms.
Come where my heart lies.
Come to my side.
For life, after all, is fleeting.
And good times are never too many.

Let us grip each other's souls for a few moments.
An embrace that will last in memory,
and carry us past Evil's grasp.

They kill with wars, with words, with smiles.

We will betray our promises to their irreverent causes.
Strike false poses,
laugh at false banners.

Tear their false messages in the darkness of the night.

Silently, we will persevere, prosper, increase,
while they curse the thoughts of the common people.
Our limbs will cross, our lips meet, our children multiply through
generations.
They will always search for new worlds to conquer.
But time is ours.

THE NEW MONEY MANTRA

Karina G. Felix

We have come a long way from the old money mindset of our parents and grand parents. The older generations grew up in an era of money scarcity and the fear of not having enough. Not having enough money, enough food, enough to pay the bills and buy clothing.

The need to hoard money became a pastime. Everyone was figuring out how and where to safeguard this money before it disappeared again.

The old money mantra was: Money doesn't grow on trees, and money is the root of all evil, is still very much deeply ingrained in previous generations and seeped into our own mind set. Breaking out of this erroneous belief takes time and constant affirmation to make the switch that would bring you to the modern day thinking of prosperity and abundance.

We now know that money is necessary. We need money to be able to live a comfortable life on a daily basis. Without money we can't have shelter; a roof over our house, we can't clothes our-selves and our loved ones, we can't feed our family let alone trying to help others in need. To become prosperous in this lifetime, one needs money to study, buy books, attend workshops and the list goes on. The old mindset was to hoard your money, now we know that we have to create money. We have to earn more money and we do this by exchanging our resources for money.

Currency such as in Energy is also used when referring to money. Money is a form of energy that must always be in circulation. If money stagnates, if you hoard your money, you will also stop the flow of money returning back to you.

Once you have dedicated your self to an education, studies in the field of your interest, experiences you've had that can be shared with others to either help them cope with the same situation or to advice not to experience the same, you will be able to use this knowledge as your source of receiving money as an exchange. This is the new direction the work field is taking. The new generation understands this at a much younger age and is finding new and creative ways to exchange their energy for money.

Creating and selling products online or selling for others while receiving a commission are all creative ways of making money. The Internet has opened up a whole new venue to do commerce and make the exchange of money as smoothly and easy as possible.

No more do we have to justify why you bought those expensive shoes. No more do you have to explain that it really is money you earned from your endeavors that is allowing you to live and enjoy life at a higher level, and that you did not do a corrupt act to be in possession of it.

We are living in a new and exiting time. Being a millionaire is becoming the norm. "Wouldn't it be nice to buy the car you *want*, instead of the car you can *afford*?" We now have the choice to make that decision.

The new money mantra is: “There is lots of money out there. Find your calling and go collect your share”.

LIGHT MY FIRE

Virginia Guido

Gather around me, everyone. Are you all sitting comfortably? Good, good. I'm going to try my hand at telling you a scary campfire story. Okay? Listen to this.

We're all familiar with the variations of the teenage couple at the cemetery, one with the escaped hook-handed serial killer, the other ending with a young man hanging from the tree over his own car, and let us not forget the undead, or the ghost of the girl celebrating her birthday.

So I'm going to have to stray from the standard setting and conjure up something new and different.

Let's start with a campground like this one here. Look around, my darlings; it's dark, and there are strange noises to be heard over the crackling of the fire. Hear them? But did you hear anything else? Shhh, listen closely. Sounds like a lost soul is calling for someone.

Do you still hear it? Oh, how sad that voice sounds. Doesn't it break your heart? Almost like a banshee wailing. Wait! Is it getting closer? Why, I believe it is. Scrunch in closer, my sweet campers. Hold hands, link arms; let's not allow this entity to break our bond. I see all your eyes wide with fear, but there is nothing to worry about as long as we are united in our goal to stay safe.

No, no, don't panic, even though it seems that the noise is

coming nearer. It's not as sad as it sounds before. Don't you think it appears angrier? I can't imagine why the tone changed like that. Perhaps we should huddle even closer. The fire is warm and chases away the dark. So let's stay here just a while longer. Okay?

No sense trying to get back to the security of our cabin. Whatever we are hearing is now between us and the trail leading back to our shelter. Fear not, my darlings, together we will be strong. I promise you all, we will get through this tonight. By morning, this horrible noise will be just a memory. You don't believe me? You think I made this up to scare you all? Now, my children, you look cynical and doubtful. We are out here alone, well, with one uninvited guest pining away. Who would I get to play such a terrible trick on you? I do not know anyone that mean. Out here, we love children. We love you all very much. Very, very much.

So my little chickens and dumplings, just sit still, continue to hold on to each other. Oh, by the way, will some of you hold these carrots? Can't you hear me over that screeching? I said, "Hold these carrots." You there, can you put some of these sliced potatoes in your pockets? I'm not sure if it will ward off the impending doom facing us, but it couldn't hurt.

Oh, my lovely little ducklings and dear lambs, don't be scared. Everyone, squeeze your eyes shut, real tight. Tighter! Do not open them until I say so. Now… just… let… me …get …up… and …move this… umph… large cauldron that has been slowly sliding down the rocky path towards us.

Perhaps you'll all feel safer if you just climb in. Say, what now? It's filled with water? That's to keep away the evil entity, honest. Are all of you inside? Great!

Now let me push this over the fire… just to keep you warm, of course.

PHILIPPINE ADVENTURE III

Margie Bonner

Marisol Village

We had been in our new home several months. The house was much larger: two bedrooms plus a maid's quarters. It was a gated community named Marisol Village. I liked the fact the gate stayed open during daytime hours, and jitneys were allowed to come and go. I did not want to miss going to the market. Within weeks, it began to feel like home. We made friends and started an active social life.

With the house came a maid named Mae. She was older than our first one, but she definitely knew the house and neighborhood well. Perhaps she had worked for the previous renter. She laughed easily. She and Cindy became pals quickly. The houses we had lived in shared one thing in common, they had cement floors painted a pleasing rust red color. Within days of our arrival, I was awakened by a waph,waph waph sound. Arriving into the living area I saw Mae, shining the floors. She was using a half shell of a coconut on her foot, making a sweeping motion, back and forth. She was as graceful as a ballet dancer; the entire scene fascinated me. In her wake, the floor gleamed. Cindy, now three, dressed in a long white nightgown, was using a smaller coconut and doing her very best to copy Mae. I soon learned this was the normal way to shine those cement floors. The oil from the coconut did the job.

We had arrived in the Philippines in 1962. A year had passed and life here was practically stress free We had adjusted to the seasons: A dry season and a rainy season no in-between. The rainy season starts in June and lasts about three to four months. I had imagined a few showers every day. Wrong. It rained every hour of every day. It seemed to me the rain came at the same speed all the time, a constant flow of water from the sky. A light bulb needed to be left on all the time in the clothes closet, otherwise mold would set in. One would think folks could become depressed, especially the American women whom I secretly thought spoiled. Not so. Nothing stopped. Kids played outside jumping in puddles, dressed in rain slickers or just their play clothes. The air was still warm, no jacket was needed. Another lesson learned.

The years we were there were the years that women wore dresses or skirts. Because of the fashions, this drew me to the downtown markets. I had discovered row after row of open air dress shops. Bolts of beautiful fabric were on display. Who could resist? I chose a shop, not really knowing what I was doing. Before I could analyze how all this worked, I found myself thumbing through a Sears Catalog. It was several years old, but within minutes I pointed to a summer dress I liked. The ladies in the shop were all smiles. My measurements were taken, and I was told to come back the next day. Imagine my delight the next day to find the dress finished. Slipping it on, it fit perfectly. My respect for the Philippine folks grew by leaps and bounds. In all honesty, I used this shop almost weekly. What lady could ever have enough clothes?

The time had come to give serious thought regarding adding to our family. We did not want Cindy to be an only child. It seemed an ideal time as the maid we employed would be a great help. In talking to our friends, I soon found out everyone had the same idea. The medical care at Clark Air Force base was top notch. Before we had any chance to second guess ourselves, I found myself with child, and a new journey presented its self. It was with faith and hope we continued our Philippine adventure

HEAT

Donna S. Fernandez

It keeps you   in shade   under the trees

the heat   of South Florida   the heat of the tropics.

Stifling.   Damp.   Scorching.

Even the memory   of the heat   from a day past

can keep you there   a long time   as you pass the time

waiting for the push   of breeze   carried on a current

like clock work   from waters   of the Atlantic.

Anticipation builds   for this breeze   to cool

to fan   to riffle   to break the heat

sure to come   again   tomorrow.

SEENAGERS

Dottie Littlefield

When Joe Morton saw Bill Logan waving at him, he stopped jogging and stood on the sidewalk across the street from Club House B in Golden Lakes.

"Are we playing pool at two this afternoon?" Bill asked as he walked up to Joe.

Joe spotted a dab of mustard on Bill's mouth. "Did you just come from Jimmy John's Restaurant?"

"No, I had them deliver the ultimate porker sandwich to the bench I was sitting on in Phase One."

Joe frowned. "Why'd you do that?"

"Because I can't afford to be seen by anyone in the restaurant who knows me, or I'd never hear the end of it from Alice. You know she has me on this stupid diet. All we have to eat is tofu, yogurt, salads, and all that other health food crap," Bill complained.

"I understand. My wife's trying to do the same damn thing to me."

Bill sighed. "I'm a meat and potatoes guy. I can't survive on that stupid stuff." He used his handkerchief to wipe the mustard off his mouth.

"Have you lost any weight by jogging every day?" Joe asked.

"No, I gained weight because all this exercise makes me

hungry."

Joe proudly patted his stomach. "I've lost five pounds. Jane bought me this red jogging suit for my birthday." He sighed. "I hinted that I'd like a new cell phone, but I got this instead because Mark West, also known as Mr. Wonderful, has one just like it. Jane told me all the women admire him."

"Admire him? They go nuts over him! He's only lived here five months, and he's dated all the single women in Phase B. No one has snagged him as a husband yet, but they're all trying. I think the longest affair lasted a month."

Joe ran his hand through his thinning hair. "I wish I had a thick head of silver hair like his."

"We can't expect miracles in our seventies. I wonder how old he is and what he does to keep looking so darn fit."

"Well for one thing, he's a bachelor and doesn't have a nagging wife who uses binoculars to watch him jog and make sure he doesn't stop to visit anyone along the way."

Bill nudged Joe. "Hey, here comes Mr. Wonderful now."
"Hey guys! How's it going?" Mark West smiled, flashing a set of perfect snow-white teeth.

Joe and Bill shook hands with him.

Bill asked, "How's your love life?"

Mark smiled and bragged "Well, I broke up with Carmen DeNiro because I fell for a beautiful willowy blonde I met at the Kravis Center last week."

Bill jabbed Joe with his elbow and murmured, "Incoming, take cover."

Mark had his back to the impending disaster and didn't see the scowling face of Carmen DeNiro as she zeroed in on him.

When Bill and Joe stepped back a few feet, Mark turned around to see what they were looking at. He gasped in surprise.

Petite Carmen glared up at him. "I got your letter today, you coward! You didn't even have the nerve to tell me in person that you're breaking up with me." She put her hands on her hips "You think you're God's gift to women. Well you aren't! You're a conceited jerk! And you had the gall to ask for me for something to remember me by. Well, here it is!" She stomped on his right foot.

He hunched forward, lifting his right foot and bringing his face within her short reach. She punched him in the nose. His head snapped back as he lost his balance on one foot and landed in a mud puddle left by the lawn sprinklers.

Carmen jutted out her chin, slapped her hands together, and shouted, "Good riddance!" She strode triumphantly to the club house.

Joe and Bill helped Mark get up and limp over to the bench. He wiped his muddy hands on his pants and sat down. He took a handkerchief out of his pocket and held it over his bloody nose. "I knew she had a temper, but I didn't think it was this bad. Do you think I'll get a black eye?"

Joe and Bill nodded, trying not to smile.

Joe looked sideways at Bill and muttered, "I forgot how dangerous being single and dating can be."

Bill glanced from Mark to Joe. "Yeah, maybe being married isn't so bad after all."

DO I KNOW YOU?

Jim Wiggins

I moved across the room of the assisted living facility to the side of the elderly lady tucked into the large lounge chair across the room. I stood next to her and asked, “Do you know who I am?

She looked pensively up into my eyes and stared for a moment in deep thought.

"I can’t think of your name,” she said, “but I know you are someone I love.” She then smiled and stretched out her arms. I bent over and gave her a hug and a kiss.

I pulled a chair over close and she leaned her head on my shoulder. I whispered softly, “Mama, I love you so much.”

Each day went pretty much the same. I had lost my Mom as I had once known her, but I had not lost her love. Mama was there and I was there. Some things can never be lost.

LET ME GO

Virginia Smythe

"Well, I finally told him. I told him to let me go — to stop calling. I'm really proud of myself, Mom" Betsy sniffs and wipes her tears. "Can you believe it?"

Mom briefly weighs the news before speaking. "Well, hon, it's about time! You've been divorced for what, 12 years now? I hope you mean what you say. How'd he take it?"

"He apologized. It was… it was… sad, and, well, just… I don't know… pathetic, really." Sighing heavily, Betsy continues, "But, mom, I'm so relieved. I think I'm getting past it now. He no longer has the power to tug at my heartstrings. And I think he heard me about respecting the boundaries I've set. Finally! I feel much lighter — maybe even free — but I'm just embarrassed that it took so long."

Betsy had been married to Tim for 14 years. *Had been.* Fourteen *loooong* years. After the sadness of ultimate rejection had lifted, Betsy felt as though she had been given a magnificent gift when he left. She hadn't even realized how unhappy she had been through the last five years of their marriage. Betsy had been too busy running on the hamster wheel of life — working 70 hours a week, climbing the corporate ladder, cooking, cleaning, seeing friends when she found the time, and all the while trying to keep her marriage together. She had never afforded herself the luxury of asking herself if she was happy. Frankly, it had never even occurred to her that there were options. Stick and stay. Fake it until you make it. Wasn't that what marriage was all about?

"So tell me what he said," pushes mom.

"Well, of course, Tim asked me for money again. But, here's the absurdity of it — this time, he told me that he'd won the lottery."

"What? The Lottery?" Mom asks incredulously.

"Yeah, Mom, it was just awful." whimpers Betsy.

"Go on," prompted mom "get it all out."

"Tim said he'd won the Lottery before he went to prison, and now he needed to borrow $400 dollars. Something about being short on his rent again. I pushed him to tell me more about his big win and why he needed money if he was now so wealthy."

Betsy tells how Tim had won 60 million dollars in the Lottery right before he went to prison.

"Yes, Mom, that's what he said. 60 million. Mil-lion. M-i-l-l-i-o-n." Betsy volleys answers to her mother's questions. Back and forth.

"Well, why on God's good green earth does he need money from you, or from anybody, if he won so much money?" Betsy's mother probes.

"I asked him those questions. Why do you need to borrow money if you're so rich? He explained he'd left his friend Eric to work on the claim prior to going to prison. Tim said that there has been a major delay with payment because the Feds think he may be a flight risk. They think he will collect his win and attempt to leave the country. I explained to him that there is a deadline for making claims to the money. And, he said Eric has it 'under control'. I asked him why he didn't just hire an attorney and he said that an attorney would take half of his windfall. He had an answer for everything."

Betsy continues to relay the conversation to her mother. "So then, I pointed out the ridiculousness of his claim. He'd won the lottery for 60 million, but won't hire an attorney because the attorney will take half. He's called his ex-wife — me — for money *AGAIN* because he cannot raise $400 for rent and he's going to be evicted. I asked if it's possible for him to survive on just half of his win — a measly 30 million. Wouldn't that suffice? Mom, he was finally stumped. That's when I told him I'd never give or loan him money again, and that I thought it was best if he didn't call me anymore.

"Any way you look at it — it's really sad. Either he's won the lottery and he's in a holding pattern waiting for payout, highly unlikely. It certainly wouldn't take eight and half years for Lotto to pay. Or he's had another break from reality, and thinks he's won but didn't. Or the most likely scenario… he needs money and he's using the Lotto story so he can try to scam people. Scam people! Scam me? This version is the one that hurts me the most. I've been so good to him." Betsy shoves back her shoulders and stands straighter.

"Yes, you certainly have," agrees Betsy's mom. "Even though you were already divorced, you continued to help him by funding his commissary account, and writing to him. And, don't forget — you gave him money when he got out too. You certainly didn't have to do any of that. You've been way more than supportive than you ever needed to be."

"Even though I told him to let me go, it doesn't really matter" sighs Betsy "this time… I've let *him* go."

TENDER NIGHT

Richard Paul Angelini

Bewitched with purity,
Sheltered in dark obscurity,
An unmatched ecstasy:

Two lovers each
For the other does reach,
Completed.

True in thought,
Tested in deed, wanting not,
Together lay contented.

In each cradled heart
A fear to part
In each, more sunsets wanted.

FREQUENT FLYER

Hartley Barnes

You look anxious. Is this your first flight? You'll be ok; relax. Flying is like sitting in your living room enjoying a horror movie, except you're thirty-nine thousand feet above the ground and moving at seven hundred miles per hour. Taking off is the riskiest part of flying: many things can go wrong, like getting a flat tire just before take-off speed, and the end of the runway is coming up. We could also fly into a flock of birds causing an engine to catch fire. But, I don't worry; I'm a frequent flyer.

Never say "bomb," or there will be a deluge of passengers all over you, beating you up. The FBI will be waiting for you to charge you with terrorism.

Turbulence is like potholes in the sky. Some are shallow, and some are deep. Flying into them can be a little frightful. You know the feeling you sometimes get in your abdomen when an elevator moves? Well, it's like that with turbulence, except its fifty times stronger. Know where the barf bag is, in case you regurgitate.

I was on a flight across the United States once. About an hour before we were scheduled to land, we flew into a storm. It was so sudden; the pilots didn't have time to take a detour. If you enjoy riding a roller- coaster, you would have loved it. At one point, we dropped ten thousand feet in less than ten seconds; you cannot imagine how exhilarating it felt. The woman seated next to me latched onto my right thigh and started to pray aloud. That's another thing; you don't do on a plane: Pray. You never pray aloud. I know, because I'm a frequent flyer. So, out of concern for the other passengers and my wife seated on the other side of me, holding my hand and shaking like a leaf, I had to tell the woman to shut up! We are not going down. The plane abruptly losing altitude did not bother me as much as where woman grasped my thigh. If we should find ourselves in a similar situation, please feel free to grab my arm. Pray, please, but to yourself.

I like window seats. I can see the clouds, the water below, and other planes zipping by. Some of them pass closer than they should. On one flight, I could look at the pilots giving the finger to the pilots of my aircraft. I believe they were from rival companies. Are you okay? You seem a little flushed.

If I'm watching television during a flight and breaking news comes on about a crash, I turn to another channel out of courtesy for others on board. Unlike me, some people get paranoid.

My wife says I should not talk about my flight experiences to the other travelers, like landing, another critical step to flying. The aircraft could go astray because of wind shear or the landing gear failing to deploy. If that happens, be calm. Hope the people sitting at the emergency exits can remember how to open the doors after we belly land.

Flying out of airports during snowstorms can be tricky. Ice forming on the wings is not a good thing. The plane has to be chemically de-iced, or the control surfaces won't work. The trick is the plane has to get off the ground before the chemical stops working. Well, if many planes are waiting to take off ahead of the one you are on, my guess is you'll be looking at your watch and thinking about tomorrow if it comes. Flying is a piece of cake. If you go to the restroom and the plane starts to dance, hurry and put things back in place and hold on. It can be a very long way back to your seat.

You do know these aircraft fly themselves with the aid of a computer. A pilot friend of mine who operates for one of the major airlines told me about a recent flight into San Francisco.

"We were on our final approach into the airport when the computer malfunctioned," he said, "Computers are the focus of pilot training, which flies and lands the planes these days."

"Yes," I said, "I could tell when the computer lands a plane— it's much smoother."

"It's not like when I learned to fly," he went on. "Today's pilots are taught how to program the computer. My co-pilot on this flight into San Francisco is one of those pilots."

"What are we going to do?" The co-pilot yelled. "What are we going to do?"

"Land on that long piece of concrete in front of us," my friend yelled back. "Now, calm the hell down and watch me and learn."

One of the flight attendants could hear the pilots talking. He banged on the cockpit door and yelled out, "Is everything alright in there?" Several of the passengers started to pray while others screamed at them to be quiet.

Can you imagine what a catastrophic accident that could have been if my friend wasn't the pilot? It's a long way down. Oh, well, I'm going to get some shuteye. Talk to you after we land. I'm a frequent flyer. I don't worry.

THE VORTEX

Don Conway

Vortex *n a whirling mass of fluid or air, especially a whirlpool or a whirlwind — a swirling vortex of emotions.*

"God Damn horse," Goodman exclaimed "it's costing me a fortune to keep, and it hasn't earned enough to pay for the hay it eats."

"That's typical for the racing business," the stable master commiserated.

Well, I'm going to find a way out of this mess Goodman thought.

The answer came about a week later when he met an alcoholic veterinarian, whose license had been revoked, at a near-by track bar. "Insurance," the Vet said over drinks provided by Goodman. "First get the horse to win some races, which makes him more valuable, and then you buy more life insurance on him. When the insurance is high enough you kill-off the horse, collect the insurance, and get out of the racing business."

"Nice idea," Goodman said, "but I see a couple of problems. First, how do I get this dog of a horse to win some races? And second: how do I kill the horse without the insurance company crying 'Murder' and refusing to pay on the policy?"

"That's where I come in — for a fee," the Vet replied. "I will supply you with a steroid cocktail, which you will give to the horse, gradually, over the next eight months. That's how he will win some races so you can add to his insurance policy. When you are ready I will give you a final, untraceable, cocktail that will burst his heart and make it look like he died of heart failure."

"Sounds illegal to me," Goodman said.

"It is," the Vet replied.

The following two days were spent in negotiating the vet's fee and detailed explanations on how to gradually administer the steroids to the horse. When Goodman was convinced the scheme was doable he began to put it into motion. The plan was to be carried out over the next ten races. It was agreed that the horse would be allowed to win six of the ten races just to justify the increase in his insurance policy.

What Goodman did not know was that the vet was burning the candle at both ends. From his years of experience at the race track, he had become acquainted with a number of professional gamblers. Once the insurance scheme was hatched he contacted "Benny Bets" Benson a well-known figure in horse racing circles. "This could be big," Benny Bets told the vet, "even after you get your cut."

A couple of days later Benny and the vet met again. "Okay, here's how it's going to go down," Benny said. "I've put together a group of big money horse players — call it a consortium — there are ten of us. We are going to place bets on this horse, even on the losing races, so no one gets suspicious. We will make money on the six races he wins. When you tell us the horse has had about all he can take we will make our big bets. The winnings, less your cut, will be divided evenly amongst the consortium members. One more thing, the owner must not know about the consortium. We don't want him to get greedy and start making his own bets. Got it?"

"Okay, I'm with you on this." The vet promised.

Johnny Fortunato was the horse's jockey. One of the things he shared with the stable manager was a genuine love of horses. At age twenty-three he had spent most of his life around them, Now, as a professional jockey, he considered himself lucky to be doing what he loved best. In the case of this particular horse, Johnny's sympathies lay more with the horse than with its owner. He knew that this horse was never going to be one of the great ones but race after race Johnny felt, he knew, that this horse was doing the best he could. Johnny could feel the courage, fortitude, and spirit this horse was pouring into every race. A bond had formed between the horse and the jockey.

As the insurance scheme unfolded Johnny sensed that something strange was happening though he was unaware of the details. By the time they got through the sixth race with three wins and three losses, Johnny was certain the horse was being doped.

He told the stable master of his suspicions who shrugged and said, "This can be a dirty business kid, keep your nose out of it and just ride the best races you can."

Goodman was satisfied with the way the scheme was playing out. So far the pattern of wins and losses had not raised any suspicions. He had purchased more insurance on the horse.

The consortium was watching the wins and losses carefully.

The vet told them that races seven and eight would be wins. Number nine would be a loss so as not to arouse any suspicions. The tenth would be a win and the final race for this horse. He would be dead before the eleventh was scheduled.

Johnny Fortunato was beside himself with concern for the horse's health. It was acting skittish and it was hard for Johnny to keep him under control. Each time they won a race the horse would go from a pre-race high to a post-race low marked by erratic behavior.

The loss of the ninth race seemed to calm the horse down somewhat. His behavior returned to normal much to Johnny's relief.

By the day of the tenth race Goodman, the consortium and Johnny Fortunato were in a swirling vortex of emotions.

Goodman was glad the scheme was coming to an end without being discovered by the Racing Commission.

The consortium placed a medium sized fortune on this race spread out over many bets. One cannot be too sure about the outcome of a horse race and they were apprehensive. So far the consortium considered itself lucky but the stakes on this race were enormous.

Johnny Fortunato knew that some sort of climax had been reached. Before the race, the horse was acting like a wild stallion. Johnny stroked him and talked to him in the tenderest tones…almost to no avail.

The tenth race started out as planned. By the halfway point around the track, Johnny and the horse started to take the lead. At the three-quarter point, they were ahead by half a length. Between the three-quarter point and the finish line, the horse started to stagger. Ten yards from the finish line the horse's front legs collapsed. It fell forward on to its chest throwing Johnny into the path of three following horses. Two of them smashed Johnny's skull with their hooves. He was dead before he realized what was happening.

By the time the ambulance reached Johnny the horse was also dead.

Because there was the death of a jockey and the unusual nature of the horse's collapse, the Racing Commission announced that there would be a thorough investigation of the incident. The post-mortem study of the horse's remains revealed an enormous amount of steroids in the horse's tissue and especially its heart.

The jockey's death was ruled an accident.

The tenth race was declared null and void and no bets were paid.

Goodman was found guilty of malfeasance, race tampering, and animal cruelty. He was sentenced to two years in prison.
The veterinarian was found dead of alcohol poisoning behind a track bar.

The members of the consortium took their losses as part of the racing life and each went their own way.

A MOTHER'S LOVE

Gloria H. Ferrara

Maria was born on January 13, 1898 in a rural area in Sicily. She was the youngest of her siblings, and had long black hair, green eyes, cheeks with a natural rose glow, and fair skin. Her life as a child was a happy one. Although she never attended school, she showed wisdom, kindness, love, compassion, and loyalty all her life.

Maria's life changed after the death of her father. When she was sixteen; she and her mother went on the long sea voyage to the United States of America. Jenny, her sibling, arranged a marriage between Maria and a cousin of Jenny's husband. The purpose of the migration to "The New World'.

Maria and her husband raised three children, and she was pregnant with their fourth. Dominic, her husband, owned and worked in a shoe repair store. Maria helped with customers; taking payments and giving change. She learned American money; distinguish each coin, and bills. Her life changed suddenly, with the murder of her husband. She left pregnant and with her three older children, the oldest ten years old; She was taken in by very close friends who cared for her and the children. And, the baby who was to be born.

Maria, with the help of her dear female friends and their families was able to live a happy life for many years. She lived in an apartment in Brooklyn, New York. The back yard directly across from hers was owned by a widower, Salvatore and four children.

Maria is my mother. Salvatore is my father. These two lonely parents of four children become friends Salvatore, called by his middle name Thomas, serenaded Maria with romantic songs from across their opposite kitchen windows. Life brought together people who were too lonely but strong in their faith. They were secure to find each other, to marry, and to add together, combined families, four more children.

MY CHILD, I FEAR THAT I WILL LOSE YOU

Judith Ann Pelio

My heart is shattered and broken.
Only God could know how much.
How many pieces have fallen to the ground?
But all have not yet been crushed beneath your feet.

My twitching eyes refuse to close,
My throat aches with unspoken words,
My voice trembles, prophetically,
I cry out, there is no sound, and no one hears.

You are dying, and I cannot stem the destruction,
For I was created to protect you, to save you.
In my mind, I see you falling,
But I am entangled and cannot catch you.

Your secrets and pain are deeply rooted,
They have not yet been revealed.
My heart, my soul, my being are terrified,
As they have been for so many years.

I wonder, what have I failed to do, to say, to notice.
You are so deeply troubled, and I am troubled, too.
I am torn with disbelief
By all the destructive things you continue to do.

My maternal hands remind me
Of the happy child I held so tightly to my chest.
A smart and beautiful child, so filled with life,
So outgoing, and loving, and so much fun.

Will the police call me about your attempted suicide, again?
Will I stand beside your stretcher in the Trauma Unit, again?
Will I search the squalid streets desperately looking for you, again?
Will you steal from me and lie to me, and do it all over, again?

Have I failed you? I will not close my eyes just yet.
You are my gift, and I unwrap you every day.
I am sorry for your pain; I would die to make you happy.
For I was created to protect you, to save you.

My life exists only at this moment,
For, my child, I fear that I will lose you.
My heart is shattered and broken.
Only God could know how much.

THE STEAK

Jim Wiiggins

Frog, named so because of his glossy bulging eyes, the curve of his lips, and the way he moved his tongue when he talked or ate, entered the butcher's shop and leaned across the counter and spoke to the butcher.

"I'm hungry for a nice big steak. Whatta' you suggest?"

A smile crossed the face of the butcher. "You're in luck. I just got in some beauties from Abe Simpleton who had a slaughtering out on his ranch yesterday. Gave me a good price, too. I'm willing to pass on the savings to you. The steaks are real doozies. He cut 'em real big. Said they were for a man with a big appetite."

The butcher then reached into the cooler, picked up a steak and dangled the biggest piece of meat in front of Frog's face that Frog had ever seen. His tongue slithered across his lower tongue, and saliva drooled from the corners of his mouth.

''HOLY MOLY" shouted FROG. "Reckon that will do. On second thought, might as well give me two of them. I've had a hankering for steak that I just can't explain."

The butcher grinned a wicked grin and said, "Good. Hope you enjoy them." He then pulled out a large sheet of butcher paper and wrapped the two steaks and slid the package across the counter toward Frog as he quoted the special price and took the money. He laughed and shook his head as Frog turned and left the building with a little hop in his gait.

When Frog got home he opened the package and took out one of the steaks. He almost slobbered over himself as he waited for the steak to get done. He quickly sat down to eat with great expectation for a delicious meal.

This damn knife. I'll have to get another one. But the *next* one didn't do any better.

By this time he realized that he had been duped by the butcher. The steak was so tough that be couldn't even bite into it.

It's like leather, he thought." Like leather." he said aloud. He mulled it over for a few minutes and then jumped to his feet. "I've got it! I'll use the steaks to replace the soles of my old shoes." He had once been an apprentice to a cobbler and hoped he could remember what to do.

He grabbed the two steaks, his two ragged shoes, and began work. He worked into the night. He breathed a sigh of relief when the job was finished and he decided to try out his shoes by taking a walk.

Early the next morning the butcher arrived at his shop and picked up the newspaper as was his custom to start the day with all the bad news. He had to blink twice. He was surprised to read the screaming headlines: LOCAL MAN ATTACKED by pack of dogs, mystery unsolved: both feet missing.

BLOWIN' THE WIND

Virginia Guido

In 1939, a legendary movie was created based on a well-known novel. A screen writer and director got together to argue and discuss changes in the script in order to garner more audience appeal. How lucky are we to find ourselves back in time as silent observers to this meeting of the minds? Let's watch how epic films are made.

Victor Fleming and George Cukor leaned over the piles of papers on the conference table. Victor claps his hands, "I'm telling you, George, *Gone with the Wind* is gonna be larger-than-life! It's got slaves, fires, wars, horses, romance, conflicts, and strong women role models like Scarlett O'Hara."

"I'm not sure, Victor. I mean slaves? Isn't that offensive? We should change them into characters who like to sing and dance."

Victor checks his notes. "What, no slaves? Okay. I'll call casting and see what they got by way of upbeat character actors. Maybe short people, like dwarves, so the viewers don't feel threatened."

"Excellent!" George gleefully replies. "Now, about the war part…our audience might be frightened by the thought of war. We have sensitive people out there. What about offering a small conflict instead?"

"I got it! We'll concentrate on Scarlett finding her way

back to her own plantation, Tara!" Victor looked as if he were on a winning streak.

"No. no, make no mention of plantations. That fills our fans with negativity. Let's just say… farm. She wants to go back to her farm. Isn't Scarlet a grown woman? That won't do for our young men. Today's boys cannot handle too much feminine pulchritude; they might get too frisky with their dates. Our star should be a young girl, vulnerable, but willing and able to be protected by those around her. You got all that?"

"Yeah, George, I got it. No sexy woman, no war, no slaves, no plantation. What about the fire, romance, and horses? I thought this movie had heart, courage, and brains."

Hmmmmm, I like the heart angle, Victor. We can also rewrite some of the scenes to include some courage. The brain part will be hard to swing because of our thin-skinned movie goers out there. They might interpret it as pertaining to them lacking intelligence. Our studio can't afford another multitudinous pizza party or play-dough giveaway to placate the masses."

"George? What if…and I'm just throwing it out there…but what if we cut the cast from hundreds of extras to just a few key people who are all searching for something? We can use the heart, courage, and intelligence as symbols for love, valor, and tolerance. Write in a witch who's involved in doing everything she can to destroy them but, of course, she's thwarted by those who know better." Victor watched as his colleague mulled it over.

"Yes! They all find out that they always had more power than they thought and, from now on, must use it wisely. Also, our little girl discovers that she's a noble true champion when it comes to helping others."

"By George, you have our movie. Though we still have a few ends to wrap up. What about the horses, can she return home on a horse?" Victor was amazed at the progress they had made.

"That is a horse of a different color, but I'll work horses somewhere in the movie, trust me. However our star should have a companion animal for her journey. Let's give her a dog, okay, Victor? Plus, I'm not crazy about the name Scarlett, too aggressive. Let's go for sweetness, something like Dorothy. I can't imagine anyone named Dorothy not being sweet, kind, and helpful."

"George? There's still one problem. The movie is called Gone with the Wind. But it doesn't seem to resemble the novel anymore. What do we do now?"

"Victor, Victor, Victor, we can still use the title. All we have to do is make a tornado to lift Dorothy from one place to another. We'll do it quickly, gently, and accompany her journey with music. Once she lands, she'll meet some little union workers who will melodiously send her on her way to salvation. Also, for every evil witch, there's a good witch who will encourage our girl to think for herself and make her own decisions. Yep, you're right, Victor, this is epic, a film for all. Come to think of it, I must be a Goddamned wizard to have written this."

NB. Victor Fleming did participate in the productions of both *Gone with the Wind* and *The Wizard of Oz*.

WHERE WOULD I BE?

Donna S. Fernandez

If the franc vs. the dollar hadn't changed
where would I be?

If French hadn't crossed to my dreams
where would I be?

If the return-home soccer flight hadn't failed
where would I be?

If I'd stayed another six months
I can't fathom where I'd be
but it might not be here.

DRIVE YOUR OWN MASERATI!

Karina G. Felix

What we hear about the millenniums is that they are entitled, selfish, impatient and lazy. We have come to this conclusion because we have a difficult time communicating with them. The real question is: are we having a harder time communicating with them or are we just having a hard time understanding them?

The new generations are challenged more and more from the second they are conceived. We start making choices for raising styles, schools, environmental, religion, friends and other "important" topics, long before the first atom split takes place.

The very conscious mother immediately starts her own regiment of eating right, not drinking, taking vitamins, exercising, spas, pampering and such. Headphones to bellies; classical music and language cd's, to give the babies a head start in intelligence and an aptitude for languages.

We spend those months tracking every single growth spurt the baby has. Regular doctor visits to listen to the heartbeat measure the head make sure it's well within the charts of gestation. Making sure it's not too big, not too small, not too round, not too skinny has all the toes, fingers, hair, and the list of details goes on and on.

Once he/she arrives on this earth, the prodding continues. Are they rolling over within the required timeframe, are they crawling, walking, drinking from a Sippy cup, laughing, playing, making friends, talking, doing math at two. The pressures and demand is non-stop.

Don't get me wrong; these measures are extremely important. We all want to be prepared for what the end results are. We live in a constant state of the future. What? When? How?

Is the baby healthy, is the baby normal, can it breathe on its own, has all the body parts been accounted for. Is there anything we need to do sooner than later? So many worries, so many concerns, so many doubts and fears.

We spend so much time creating this amazing environment for our babies; yet flood them with constant fear, doubts and concerns during their most developmental stages.

These fears, doubts, concern and worry goes on long into adulthood. At what point do we stop the doubts and fears, and switch it to belief, trust and empowerment: Never really. At least not until overwhelm takes hold of us and we have to take a step back. And this is mostly to give us a break.

From the moment the baby is born, we pamper them and spoil them. We give them what they want, whether to make them happy or to give ourselves some peace.

That's the real question! Who is making whom happy? They have to be extremely behaved, especially in front of family and friends, and they have to be the smartest in class and in school. They have to play sports so we can cheer them on the sideline next to the other parents. They must attend the best school, best church, best extracurricular, best clothing, best friends, best neighborhoods and the list goes on and on.

And these kids perform. They work hard. They get the good grades. They excel at their extracurricular activities, they behave in public and then they also learn early on how easy it is to make mommy and daddy happy.

They learn how to manipulate these same people to get what they desire. And where exactly did they learn these skills? Well, where else. Haven't we been manipulating them their whole lives?

We manipulate, convince and bribe them their whole lives. They generally work hard during those initial years, and then they leave the comfort of the home, and go into the school system that ups the ante with threats, punishments and insecurities.

They work as hard as they can for as long as they can survive and then teenage years kick it, and there's a standstill, a picket line of strikers refusing to go on any longer within those demands. The drive, the expectations and the goals they need to reach are really not their chosen paths, but ours –the parents.

Now would be a good time for us as parents to stop and ask the question: What would you like? What does your future look like to you? Is there something specific you'd like to be doing?

But our old habits and belief systems keep us trapped in the world of "What would my parents do?". What would my parents, friends, neighbors say, think, believe about me?'. This is where we get stuck.

We have demanded so much, so fast, from our millenniums that we never took a moment to not only give them a say, but also just listen to what they have to say.

Our Millenniums have been created as a new computer model and processing system, we have no clue how to use.

We put so much onto them that now they just need a break, to figure out what is really out there for them. We are not the conductors of their trolleys. We must step back and let them take the wheel. Some may jump behind a Ferrari, while another thinks a hybrid is more their style, but whatever vehicle they choose to continue their journey on, we should be there as guides, mentors and advisors. The raising part is over.

Now go drive your own Maserati!

THE LILY WEED

Richard Paul Angelini

Like a lost child I wandered
Past bright, pink and verdant green growing
Against concrete, heat, and wheels, by the road.

I passed a fearless struggle.
Cars sped by, driven by desire and arrogance,
And yet through concrete green leaves thrust up
Offering a resplendent bouquet to the sun.

With desperate profusion the weed prospers
In a singularly beautiful world,
Ambivalent to the danger near.

In only a crack it feeds and blooms,
Consumed with a need to re-create its' own kind.
It worries not about the future,
Refuses man's decrees,
And gives its' children out to chance.

It spites man's designs.

Like the Lilies Of The Field,
The weed lives and thrives in a truth
We are always re-discovering.

It obeys only Nature..

PHILIPPINE ADVENTURE IV

Margie Bonner

Great Changes Occurring:

The year 1963 promised to be an exciting one. Our baby was due to arrive in mid November. We were settled in our new home. Mae, our maid, proved to be a godsend; she seemed to know what was needed, before we did. I had become comfortable with the team of doctors who would see me through my pregnancy. Little did I know this would be a year not soon forgotten. Several months into the new year, my husband received a temporary duty assignment. He was being sent to Thailand for at least three months. This caused a set of problems. The car we owned had a stick shift, which I could not operate, but we had met a couple who soon became our best friends. They had a daughter the same age as Cindy' and we spent numerous weekends together. It was with their support that I felt perfectly safe.

Life and times in the Philippines were tranquil. The mood of the residents remained calm, and the few newspapers I read did not speak of uprising or dire predictions of the future. I still felt the government was very lax in the upkeep of the towns I travelled in. Open sewage was visible in most of the back streets, and animals roamed about freely causing even more odor and confusion. Traffic was nonstop with the jeeps and the horse drawn celestas. This was all normal to me by this time, and I paid little attention.

Time went by, and I had no difficulty with my pregnancy. The months my husband was gone passed quickly. He soon returned with some goodies for Cindy and me. Thailand is noted for precious gems. He bought home two rings. One was called the Princess ring. It was gold with tiny different colored stones piled on top of each other. This ring was definitely a show stopper.

The due date I had been given was mid November. My husband felt it wise to take his thirty day leave from work to be available if I should need him. I remember well those thirty days. Each day he looked at me with questioning eyes; each day I shook my head. I felt great with no aches or pains.

On Nov. 22 we drove to the Base-Exchange for a bit of shopping. I was waddling about oblivious to how I looked, because, in truth, I was enormous. Suddenly, over the loud speaker, a message came forth. The U.S. president John F. Kennedy had been shot and killed in Dallas, Texas. I shall never forget the utter silence that fell over that store. My husband came toward me, reaching for my hand, he said, "Lets go home."

The week that followed was not happy. We both wanted to go to our real home, to share in the deep sorrow of our country. The little black and white TV that we owned was on night and day as we tried to make sense of the happenings in the U.S.

The thirty days was up, and my husband went back to work. Cindy and I continued our day to day routine. On December third, we walked to a nearby beauty shop that we used frequently. Cindy had her nails done and her tiny little toes polished. It was always a big decision to choose the perfect color. The girls at the shop fussed over her.

Walking home that morning, I marveled, at what a beautiful day it was. Suddenly without warning, my sandals slipped on loose gravel and I fell, completely and fast right on my bottom. It happened so quickly, I was dazed. I looked around and didn't see a soul. I could feel Cindy's hands tugging on my blouse saying in a frantic voice, "Get up Mommy, I will help you." I did not want her to cry, so I told her to wait just a bit and I would get up. Somehow, I managed to get on my knees and was able to stand. When I stood up, I did not feel any pain, and we slowly made our way home.

Within an hour, we were lying together in bed. She was sound asleep beside me. I had been feeling back pain since lying down and knew something was happening. I told Mae to get me a jitney as I needed to go to AC's house. AC was our friend. His real name was Archie, but he was known to all by this nick name. I knew he was home and had a car Mae did as directed. AC came rushing from the house, not even taking the time to comb his hair. He helped me in his car and within minutes we were on our way to the hospital. The pain was unrelenting. I could feel waves of anxiety coming from AC. I did my best to hide the discomfort I felt and did not make a sound.

Suddenly the car began to sputter. AC pulled to the side as the car slowly stopped. He looked and acted frantic. I was numb with crazy thoughts coursing through my mind. "Dear God, am I staring in a sitcom. "What more could happen?" AC grabbed a gas can and ran. I saw him through the windshield running as fast as his short legs would go. I continued to press against the passenger door, making sure it was locked as I could visualize myself tumbling out.

Time seemed to float away from me as I felt nothing except what was occurring inside of me. He soon returned, and the next thing I remember was him helping me into the hospital. He patted me on my shoulder and said, "I will go find Neal" my husband. The nurses began to undress me, but soon stopped and said "Get her into delivery"

Our baby girl was delivered, washed, weighed, and wrapped in a cozy pink blanket before my husband arrived. Later we marveled that both she and I were fine when so much could have occurred to damage us both: first the dangerous fall, then the mad rush to the hospital. So much could have happened but none did. We were thankful.

I and the baby, whom we named Jo Ann, stayed in the hospital for seven days. This was due to the over precautions of infections in the new-born. Having us both back home was pure joy for all of us, especially Cindy.

Within two months we, made our final move. We were assigned a house on base. This house was very large and made out of wood. The only familiar thing was the rust colored cement floors. The maid's quarters were beautiful. We all were so fond of Mae that we celebrated together.

Paper work was on going. JoAnn was issued a Philippine birth certificate along with paper work to file for her U.S. certificate. Our feelings were a jumble. We wanted to go home, yet we would miss our life abroad, our friends, and especially Mae. I waited every day for my husband's transfer orders.

They came. We were being sent to Nellis Air Force Base, in Las Vegas. Wow! What a change. The following weeks were very busy, and when Josie (by this time I had given her a nickname] was eight months old we flew home. One item of note, disposable diapers had been invented. What a lifesaver for the traveler.

The day we left the Philippines was bitter-sweet. Climbing the stairs into the huge jet, again with a baby in my arms, seemed natural but so much more relaxing because right behind me was my husband and our oldest daughter. Together our family looked forward to the next adventure as we waved good bye to the Philippine Islands.

BILLY AND ROCKY

Hartley Barnes

Billy and Rocky are the elders on a small farm in the center of New York City. They both joined the other animals in December 2009. Coexisting is difficult because of their domineering personalities. Rocky, a Cubalaya rooster, speaks Spanish, is self-centered, and at times is obnoxious. Billy, a Ram goat is assertive and cantankerous with a twist; he has an iPod hanging from his neck with headphones, and he listens to sixties music. He is selective when it comes to food and hates it when Rocky stereotypes him.

"You eat anything, don't you? Goats are not discriminate when it comes to food, Senor." Rocky's favorite thing to say when he wants to upset Billy.

Rocky is not a fan of the cliché "the early bird gets the worm." He wakes up every morning at five thirty, crows for five minutes, then goes back to sleep. The crowing doesn't bother the other animals, except Billy.

"He deliberately crows to upset me," Billy grumbled. "One day I'll sneak up on him while he's taking a nap, and glue his beak together. When he tries to crow, he'll blow himself up."

"Buenos Dias, Lilly," Rocky shouted from his roost.

Billy, looking up yelled "Don't say anything to me, bird brain. How many times do I have to tell you my name is Billy? Billy! Billy! — you little twerp!"

Rocky looks up, down, side to side and behind, "Who are you referring to, senor?"

"Is someone up there with you, you ignoramus?" he shouted at Rocky.

Rocky flies to the ground, "You woke up on the wrong side of the barn today, senor Lilly…Billy."

"Yes, because of the stupid noise you make every morning."

"It is not noise, hombre."

"How dare you address me as such, you foul despicable bag of feathers."

"What's your problema?"

"I have been storing foods in a secret location for my birthday, and it's missing." Billy is standing up on his hind legs as if he is going to lunge at Rocky, "Give it back!"

"What?" replied Rocky, and bellowed a crow.

"My food, my birthday food, I want it back and now!"

"I don't steal. I'm royalty."

"What part of you? You sashay like it, but you're not!"

"I don't know what you are talking about, amigo," Rocky said sarcastically.

"You know I don't like when others touch my food. Give it back, or I will inform the chickens of your philandering ways."

"That's hitting below the belt, my friend."

"You don't wear trousers—you Insidious soon–to–be someone's drumsticks."

"Por favor, that is not very nice."

Rocky flies back to the roost. He knows Billy is close to losing his temper whenever he starts to bleat and paw at the ground.

"I resent your accusation; I don't eat what you eat."

"You don't eat. You don't have teeth—kaleidoscope—you swallow."

"This is outrageous, you accusing me of thievery." He lights a cigar. "In the old days, I would fight you to protect my dignity." Rocky is now pacing on the roost; he lets out a cloud of smoke. "If you persist, I will be forced to take logical action."

"Legal— you babbling fool."

"I will not tolerate any more insults, senor Goat. Logical! Meaning to do something that makes sense to quell your yapping. You want to be on someone's dinner table? Senior, keep talking."

"Chickens, chickens, gather around," Billy is yelling as loud as he can. "I have news."

Rocky flies to the rock. "My gracious friend, we can work this out. I don't know anything about your food; I will help you find it, promesa, promesa, si, si."

"It's my last birthday here; I want my food—I have to celebrate."

"Senor, your food is not important to me. What do you mean, last birthday?"

"My birthday is four days away, that's how much time you have to return my food, or you will pay."

"I don't like what you just said, my sure-footed friend."

"We are not friends!"

Shaking his head vigorously, causing his headphones to slip over his ears, as he starts to bob his head up and down, he walks off looking back. “Four days.”

“Or what senor?”

“Can you fly without tail feathers.” Climbing atop his favorite rock, he relaxes, and starts to chew his cud. Rocky has not taken his eyes off him; he’s trying to figure out what Billy is up to.

I’ll go ask the chickens; all they do is scratch for food and gossip. They’ll know. Rocky decides not to walk, fearing Billy might try to hurt him. He flies to a tree in the area where the chickens are.

“Saiddy,” Saiddy snaps back at him, “don’t talk to me, and don’t say anything to the rest of the girls. If you think you are going to try and fertilize any eggs today, think again— you charlatan!”

“What! Who do you think you are addressing, Senorita? What’s the problema?

“Go ask those chicken heads next door, you counterfeit. We know where you have been spending your time after dark.”

“Billy!” He flies back to his roost and starts crowing as loud as he can. I’ll show him, that rat! After a half hour, Billy hasn’t responded. I know he can hear me, he’s trying to ignore me, or, damn, he must have his headphones on. There goes my effort. No, I’ll go to him, Rooster to Goat; I can’t let him defame my impeccable character because he’s got issues. Rocky flies to the rock, Billy is sleeping. Rocky pecks him and launches himself to the nearby tree. Billy leaps to his feet, and looking around while shak-

ing his head, the headphones slide on to his neck, "Who hit me?"
"Me, senor."
"You lost touch with reality? Hitting me is not acceptable."

"Neither is losing my tail feathers and my harem." He descends to the ground. "Come down here. Now! We must talk." Billy doesn't respond. "Senor Lilly!"

"Billy! You halfwit!—I'm not interested in your polygamous lifestyle. Do you have my food?"

"Hmmmmm! The pot calling the kettle black; we must talk."

"Why do I tolerate you?"

"Why do you blame me for everything that goes wrong in your life? You misplace your headphones, and you said I took it because you wouldn't let me listen to salsa."

"It wouldn't have worked anyway. Your head is too small."

"Oh, that's funny, and all the other things, like— the canopy you erected over your rock. You accused me of knocking it down, when it was the wind."

Billy gets in Rocky's face; Rocky does not move. "Stop the whining!"

"You told the girls I've been fooling around."

Billy spins around and jumps about five feet away with his back towards Rocky.

"Is that what they told you?" Rocky doesn't answer. "Well?"

"I. . ." realizing he assumed Billy told them.

Billy whirls around. "You ingrate!" He jumps on the rock.

So, you didn't, Sir Billy?"

"No, where is my food?"

"I don't know, I didn't take it—what's wrong? I'm trying to figure out what's going on with you. I apologize for pecking you." Billy leaps off the rock and lands in front of Rocky, Rocky takes a step backwards. "I will understand if you care to discuss your problem with me, please senor . . . let me help."

"Haven't you noticed I'm the only goat left on the farm? I suspect all the others have been curried."

As a matter of fact, you are, and I'm the only rooster, except for that young one I've been keeping my eyes on. He struts around likes his poop don't stink. I've been so busy with the young ladies, I didn't notice– Oh, so you are next to be curried," Billie's mouth fell open. "I mean–you think you are next."

Sitting on his back legs like a dog, he sinks into despair. "What am I going to do?"

Rocky moves closer. "I will never be someone's drumsticks like you said. I'm too old; my meat is tough. What I'm saying is—I've been around a long time, and not by accident. I used to wake up in the mornings wondering if I will be the next one to grace the dinner table. I worried so much. If I were human, I would be taking Prozac. I couldn't see myself in hot oil, not that I would feel anything, so, I made myself invisible, out of sight, out of mind."

Billy stands up and steps towards Rocky. "Go away. You are trying to trick me into believing you care what happens to me."

"I do, Senor."

"No!"

"Si!"

"Stop it, I said! A rooster can't care about a goat; we are not of the same feathers."

"You don't have feathers, silly. When I look at you, I see a friend."

"You're delusional."

"Your meat is tough, too— and it stinks."

"Don't. Call me stink?"

"Sorry, I mean gamey."

"How would you know? You don't consume meat."

"That's what you think. At your age, you won't be anybody's cuisine, that's what we have in common. Why do you think we are not polarized? We are in the same canoe."

Billy climbs to the top of his rock and lies down with his legs under him. "I want to be alone; I have to decide where I will go." He let out a bleat.

"If you leave, who will I fight with, senor?"

"We are on a cosmopolitan farm, it's your choice."

"Only the girls and you understand me."

"So, why haven't you told them about your problem?"

"Problem?"

"Why you can't fertilize their eggs."

"How did you know?"

"The girls you visit at night next door told me of your difficulties, while they laughed. I told them to stop it; it's not your fault, as I tried not to laugh along with them."

Rocky is getting emotional. "You were defending me."

"No! I wanted them to stop; the frequency of their voices hurt my ears."

"You care about me, too, don't you?"

"No! Go and get my food!"

"OK, senor, I will." As he walks away, Billy calls to him. "Wait, you said you didn't take my food."

"Yes, that's what I said. Excuse me."

This is interesting. How is he going to find food that doesn't exist.

It's early morning on Billy's birthday, Rocky did not crow.

"Here is your food; I forgot the cerveza."

"It's not my food."

"I know— happy birthday, amigo."

"Have you looked around here lately, Rocky? Our age sets us apart; the sun is setting for us. Why are we still here?"

"We were useful, senor."

"Si, as you would say. We produced, and we propagated our respective kind."

"That is how we survived, amigo."

"We served a purpose," Billy let out two bleats.

"Si senor, we did our duty." Rocky looks up to the skies, and he takes a deep breath. "Yah . . . we are alone Billy. The youngsters are so fixated with electronics they don't see us. The owners of the farm got what they want, and the rest, the not so young, don't have time for us. We cramp their style."

"Now, Rocky, do you understand why I'm worried about the dinner table, I don't want a knife and fork to fight over me."

"I 'm just an old foul that wants to live a little more—I need you— happy birthday, Billy, my friend."

"I need you too; I'm just an old goat who wants to live forever." Moving to the other side of the rock, Billy calls Rocky,

"Come and see what I have." Rocky comes around to see a big pan with two straws; it's filled with beer.

"Drink up, to what's ahead."

"No problem, amigo."

They both assume a relaxing position. "Why did you lie about the food?"

"I'll tell you tomorrow. Why didn't you crow this morning?"

"I'll tell you tomorrow."

A GOOD MISSION

Don Conway

Novgorod, USSR, November 22, 1944. 4:30 a.m.

Senior Lieutenant Lilya Alexandrovna Belochkin, the pilot, and her crew of four women had been waiting in their Tupolov-2D since 4:00 a.m. At the mission briefing, the pilots were told to, "Wait for the white flare. That is your signal to proceed with the mission." It was cold, and there was no provision for heat in these new Tupolov's. There were two thermos bottles of tea, but she knew the crew would need them later in the flight. So they were all cold, herself, her co-pilot, the navigator and the two gunners. She and her crew were one of forty-six all-women crews on active duty in the Air Force.

It has been difficult she thought. *Ever since she enlisted in 1941 right after Hitler declared war on the USSR, there had been the usual insults and humiliations from the male officers. No separate living quarters for women, no separate toilets. Not even uniforms for women. They had to make do with male uniforms. But we persevered, she thought, and here we sit, waiting to take off on our eleventh mission.*

So much for male prejudices!

As she sat thinking, her mind reminisced about her flying career. In 1930 at fifteen she joined a flying club. She started flying for the mail service in 1936. By 1941, she had been flying for commercial services for five years. The Air Force was happy to get her.

The white flare jolted her out of her revere. Time to go.

The Tupulov was a temperamental machine. On landings, one had to watch the angle of decent very carefully and hold it within three or four degrees. Taking off with three thousand pounds of bombs, as she was doing now, required a long run at full power to get it up to flying speed. Crosswinds were no help.

Once they were airborne, and information with the other eighty-seven planes, it was critical to hold her position in the formation since each plane was responsible for protecting the rear of the plane ahead.

She reviewed her course, flying speed and the weather with her navigator. One hour and twenty-two minutes to the target area in Lithuania. , The Pilots were told at the briefing that the area was a marshaling point for German forces getting ready to retreat into Germany. They were also told that the weather over Lithuania was deteriorating.

Twenty minutes out from the target area, the weather had gotten dangerous. The entire squadron would have to descend to 850 meters (2,700 feet) to make their bombing runs. This made them much more vulnerable to the German anti-aircraft guns. Lilya wished they were able to go in at their normal altitude of 1000 meters (3200 feet) where they were much safer.

Two minutes from the target she descended to 850 meters and started her bombing run. Suddenly, the plane in front of her disappeared. It simply vanished, and they were alone in the sky. She continued on course. Thirty seconds later the plane jolted sharply to the right and up about fifty feet. They'd been hit! Fragments of the shell grazed the left engine, entered the cockpit, and hit Lilya in the underside of her right thigh.

Of course, there was pain, but the realization of what had happened, and her fight to regain control of the aircraft overcame the initial pain. *I've got to get us out of here* was all she could think of. Since the plane was thrown to the right, she instinctively went with it and did a climbing one hundred and eighty-degree turn. Once they reached 2500 feet and headed back towards Russia, she was able to take stock of their situation. The airplane was flyable with one engine, but that was not the problem. The problem was her. She was losing blood from her wound.

"I cannot make it back to Novgorod." Lilya told her navigator. "Find us an alternative landing field nearby." Moments later the navigator told her there was a fighter base at Povno, about twenty minutes away. Lilya changed course and headed for it.

When they got to Povno, they were told that the fighter squadron was in the middle of taking off and that she would have to circle the field until the air was clear…about ten minutes.

By the time they were cleared to land Lilya was dizzy and light headed from loss of blood. Getting the Tupulov on the ground in her condition, and with just one engine, was terrifying and pushed her flying skills to the limit. Once on the ground, her co-pilot was able to taxi the plane off the runway. Lilya shut down the remaining engine and realized that her crew was safe, she had saved the airplane, and she was not going to die. *All-in-all* a successful mission she thought as she collapsed into unconsciousness.

ME TOO

Judith Ann Pelio

You beat me hard and threw me down,
You raped me till I cried.
You stole my things and punched my face,
Then left me there to die.

My life was changed in many ways
That you will never know.
I crawled, I climbed, I stood up straight,
My scars they did not show.

My body healed, I walked again,
As time moved slowly past,
Those memories will be erased,
I'll fight so they don't last.

I've worked so hard that I'd be strong
In spirit and in mind.
Now I'll be ready when you come.
Much stronger you will find.

The day has come, I started new,
I've gone to every length,
So that I'd stand amazed and grand
To celebrate my strength.

I've learned a newfound sense of love
For my life and for ME.
I am renewed and quite improved
To live, to thrive, to Be.

So when you need to beat and rape,
To prove your force and might,
Remember US, you spineless wuss,
MeToo will win THAT fight!

LIFE IS A CIRCLE

Shanda N. Whittle

I was born in the foothills of the Rocky Mountains in Colorado, near the Garden of the Gods, on the eve of a new year, to a free-spirited twenty-year-old mother. As soon as she had turned eighteen in 1972, she dropped out of high school, ran away from the sheltered Irish/Italian home she had been adopted into as an infant, and went on a journey to find herself and a place where she "belonged." What she found after hitchhiking from Buffalo, New York, to the Haight-Ashbury district of San Francisco was my father, a purple-heart, combat-medic veteran fresh off a plane from Vietnam.

Traits of resiliency and compassionate, empathic caring were ingrained in me as a child and young adult. Emotional Intelligence was unlocked in me through my first twenty-seven years of life as a child of mentally-ill parents, as an adolescent patient disabled by intractable temporal lobe epilepsy, and as a twenty-five-year-old patient diagnosed with a brain tumor.

Resiliency and empathy grew inside of me as an adolescent and young adult. They created a beautiful garden of compassion in a life that was dark and full of fear. By the time I graduated from high school, I had been told I'd never be able to drive, go to college, live on my own, or have children. My illness raged through my brain, creating thunderous storms my neurologist was unable to control. Once high school ended, my fate loomed dark and ominous in my thoughts. The closer I got to the end, the more I felt the walls of my life closing in on me, crushing my hopes and dreams, bringing thoughts of suicide to my mind.

Fortunately, my life was set on a different path thanks to discoveries made during our country's first "Decade of the Brain". I entered a research study when I was nineteen and became one of the first patients in the country to undergo a new type of surgery for my type of epilepsy. I learned how to drive when I was twenty-one and was finally given the chance to go to college. I knew I wanted to join a profession that helped others - my initial choices being social work or psychology. I changed my mind after my uncle, a social worker, introduced me to the nursing shortage that was rapidly increasing in our country during the mid-1990's.

I entered the field of nursing wearing my heart and my past on my sleeve. In thinking about this and looking back to when I entered nursing school in 1996, I wore my past in much the same way Nathaniel Hawthorne described in his book The Scarlet Letter. This wasn't because I was born out of wedlock, but because my illnesses and family situation were filled with social stigmatization and led me to feel shameful and depressed. This was all started by the mosquito-borne illness I acquired at the age of eight months old while living in Boulder, Colorado.

In 2000, during the summer before my last year in nursing school, I was diagnosed with a brain tumor in the center of my brain and began having thoughts of writing a book about my past journey that led me into nursing. At that moment in time it was a thought I had to leave my "legacy" given my poor health. Following surgery and treatment of this tumor, I went back to nursing school and played with the idea of writing my story every now and then.

Upon graduating from nursing school and becoming licensed as a registered nurse, many of my classmates followed the recommendation of our nursing school and entered areas of medical-surgical nursing. It was a recommendation made to ensure we would get more experience before we decided on a specialty field. This was a decision I didn't need to make. I had entered nursing school knowing I wanted to care for the most vulnerable populations in our healthcare system. This desire of mine came from my early experiences as a patient that had left me vulnerable to the abuses of others when I was unable to defend myself.

My early work as a registered nurse was devoted to caring for patient populations with Alzheimer's Disease, end-stage AIDS, and brain injuries. This work tested my resiliency and introduced me to the extent of unfortunate stigma in our healthcare system. My heart was heavy with empathy for these patients. I felt their plight of hopelessness and silent despair because it had once been mine.

This work led me into the field of mental health where I care for one of the most vulnerable patient populations in our healthcare system. It is here that seedlings of my early experiences as a child and patient began to grow and spread in the garden of compassion I had once hidden and nurtured as a means for survival. The result of this growth and my experiences give me the ability to see and care for my patients as whole beings.

In the spring of 2018 I traveled home to Boulder, Colorado where my story began in 1974. It was there that I started my journey to become a Caritas Coach with the well-known nurse theorists: Dr. Jean Watson. Dr. Watson talks about writing as a way to learn about herself and to express what she needs to express. I used to feel uncomfortable speaking about my illnesses and time as a patient, but it's an anxiety I overcame by writing a book about these experiences and how they brought me into nursing. It wasn't until I moved to Florida in 2013 and joined the Royal Palm Beach Writing Group in 2014 that I got serious about writing it with the support, love, and encouragement of my new writing family. After 14 years of thinking about writing this book to tell my story, it only took me three years with my loving writing family to write it and today it's with a publisher in the process of being published.

Florence Nightingale identified nursing as a "calling". This is something I believe to be true. I had no idea who Dr. Jean Watson was when I entered nursing school, but I feel as if her caring energies are what guided me into the field of nursing to fulfill my "calling" and home to Boulder in 2018, bringing my story of healing full circle. Like the moon, I may shine bright one night, but may be covered and hidden the next; I may be full and whole some days but may be small and weak another. But one thing is for sure every day and every night. Like the moon, I will always be there, and with Dr. Watson and my new Caritas Coach family, I'll always be there with a mindful, caring presence, and a heart filled with light, love, and compassion; no matter what, to listen, understand, accept, help, and heal others who need help and healing as I once did.

TELL HER ABOUT IT

Virginia Guido

Robin was a very clever girl in many ways. Even at five years old, she knew the value of a promise. As a child she was frugal, saving the coins she would find while on the beach or in the park. One time, her brother, whom she adored, wanted to borrow a dollar from her. Although he assured her he would repay her, Robin asked him to give her something he cherished to hold until she got her dollar back.

"A promise is a promise," she reminded him

When Robin grew up, she pursued a law degree and graduated at the top of her class. Many prestigious firms contacted her, but Robin chose to be a Public Defender. She was fluent in four languages, an advantage in this field. Her reputation as a ruthless PD was stellar. Prosecutors feared Robin while criminals worshipped her.

*****

"Hey, Jerry, listen to me. Jerry, you got to ask for this chick to defend you. She never loses." The two young men sat at the police precinct, handcuffed to chairs, thinking about their imminent fate.

"I dunno, man. This is bad. Really bad." Jerry shook his head sadly.

"No, I swear she's good. She got my cousin, Michael, off

with no time served. It's like she's magic or something, y'know?" Charlie could be very persuasive.

"How do I get her?"

"Let me think." Charlie scratched his head with his free hand. "You got rights. You tell them that you don't speak good English and you need someone who speaks your language. The cops will bring her into you. They always call for her. You don't even have to know her name."

"You sure?"

"Yeah. You can ask my cousin, Michael, if you can find him. He disappeared right after he was let go. Who knows where he is now?"

Jerry looked up from his seat and called to the arresting officer, "Hey you! I need a public defender, but I got a language problem."

*****

"So tell me, honestly, are you guilty? Did you do what the cops say you did? Don't lie to me." Robin looked intently at Jerry from across the table in the interrogation room.

Jerry stared at the petite blonde, debating whether or not he should tell the truth. "Yeah, I did it. You can see it on video. It's probably all over the internet by now. You got to be one hell of a lawyer to get me out of this."

She waved her hand as if to dismiss his statement. "Don't worry about the video. For every incriminating capture on film, there's another contesting one in cyberspace. Let me worry about that."

He sat back in his chair, slightly more relaxed than before but still worried. Jerry was certain that he would spend a long time behind bars. *How was she gonna convince a jury that he was innocent of murder?*

*****

"Ladies and Gentlemen of the jury, if you examine the video closely, you'll notice that the killer's face is not discernible at all. In addition to my client, how many people fit the physical features of the person in the video? Look around this courtroom, and you'll see several right here. Could you presume that anyone of them is guilty of this murder?"

Robin leaned in closer to the jury, "This is a grainy low resolution film that is not continuous. It appears to be edited. Any intelligent person would question the validity of using this as evidence."

Her banter, knowledge, and charm always swayed the jury in her favor. However, there was another reason why she never lost. Robin and her staff would stay up nights going over testimonies, reviewing evidence, searching for loopholes or slip ups that might have occurred during the arrest or investigation. She was definitely the prosecutor's nightmare.

*****

Jerry hugged his family and stuck his tongue out at the victim's family. He was free! A minor technicality had released him from a guilty verdict and serving time in prison. *This bitch is the best, and she didn't cost me a penny.*

He showed no remorse for his actions and didn't even

thank Robin. *Par for the course*, she thought. *They never say thanks because they don't care about anyone else.*

*****

Sipping her glass of Cabernet Sauvignon, Robin looked up to see the waiter approaching.

"I'm sorry to interrupt your dinner, Madam, but a young man informed me that you dropped your wallet."

She studied the expensive designer wallet and held out her hand to receive it. "Why thank you, sir. I would've been lost without it."

Robin opened the wallet, counted the bills, smiled, and read the enclosed card: "Thank you for all your help." This note of gratitude was appreciated but not necessary.

The family of the victim had been guaranteed that Jerry would no longer be a threat to anyone- anywhere- anymore. Robin's "staff" had taken care of that.

This time the video recording of Jerry was so clear there would be no doubt as to his identity as he was executed.

She was a great public defender. As long as you admitted your guilt, Robin could get you off, but there was a higher price to pay: the perpetrator's life for a handsome fee paid by the victim's relatives.

Ever since the death of her brother, she promised to punish his killer and others like him. Her beloved brother was lying in a grave while his cold-blooded killer, Michael, enjoyed working out at the prison gym, conjugal visits with his favorite females, and other perks from the inmates. She offered to appeal his case, knowing she would win, thus setting him free. From that point, it was easy to avenge her brother's death.

Still, Robin had criteria as a public defender: 1. Approach the victim's family, explain your strategy. 2. Make sure your client admits to being guilty but shows no regrets. 3. Win your case. No problem there; her staff was ruthless- they paid off witnesses and jury members, tampered with evidence, and erased segments of videos. 4. Employ your minions to carry out justice. 5. Collect your legal fee, although she would have gotten revenge for free.

Yes, Robin was a clever girl in many ways.

OLIVIA JEAN

Donna S. Fernandez

Can you imagine
on the day you were born
    the earth was green
    the sky was blue.

My thoughts spun
to the pitter-patter of lyrical verse.
Longfellow's "The Children's Hour" came to mind,
and how you had "plotted and planned…to take us
    by surprise."

A rush into the world,
and over the telephone wire,
your Great Auntie
heard your first cries.
Liberation?
Jubilation?
    A little of both, perhaps.

This Great Auntie lives down South
    I mean
        really down South,
and wonders what you will collect.
Dolls, string, floating boats,

maybe even trains.
Or will it be dried-up leaves,
or music notes,
or all creatures great and small.

You need to know
that in the mix
I cross my fingers
and hope
you will collect books
and a few pieces of art.

Know this
Field wishes you to sail "off in a wooden shoe"
with Wynken, Blynken, and Nod.
Stevenson hopes
you go up in a swing,
"up in the air so blue."
And Yeats wants for you to catch
"a little silver trout."

While, I, your Great Auntie
who lives way down South
Just wants, for now,
to see your newborn
flaxen hair.

A WHIRLWIND OF LOVE

Karina G. Felix

She can't believe the amount of pain she experienced by missing someone at this magnitude. She realized a bit too late that the feelings she had for him was more than just lust and games. She fell for him and she fell hard.

Her heart aches thinking of him. She smiles still, when recalling images and conversations they had. She can still see the desire in his eyes and feel the passion in his kisses. The warmth of his body against hers and how he moved once he was inside of her.

Their embrace alone would be the prelude of what's to come. The way their bodies just melted into each other, she, always feeling like she will lose her footing and feeling faint.

He always strong and ready for that total surrender, would hold on even tighter to her waist and crush her body to his, slightly picking her off the floor, while she still made a slight effort to keep her toes on the ground for balance.

She loved everything about him, especially his smile. So much want, so much need, then one day all gone. Where did it go? She is still searching for answers. She misses him, but does he miss her? She will never know, or will she?

It all started out so innocently, never looking for love or companionship. They where both caught up in a whirlwind of love that will leave her forever wondering if she will ever experience such deep feelings for anyone ever again.

NOW NOT

Richard Paul Angelini

How many loves are lost in the grime of Now's tread?
The torn track in mud?
The worn story yet only just passed?

Tall oaks and sycamore capture nourishment from her tears.
Daisies gather the shade from her crouching silhouette.
She takes a clover, then another,
and releases them to the breeze with a gentle breath.

They had once kissed, loved.

She looked for compassion,
understanding,
hidden in Nature's quiet pause from the bustling city.

Gloom crept from her shadow to her pale face,
trembled her hands and bent her over as if carrying the dead weight
of a dead dream.

She melted into the field,
down,
her sarcophagus of flower willing.

She would take her own life.

"It is nothing really, anymore," she whispered.

"Just a shell,

blank inside and fading with sunset.

Once he was.

Now not."

A MONOLOGUE FOR MY DOG

Hartley Barnes

I have learned to trust you, resulting in a friendship that is extraordinary. You have given me many special moments. You have opened my eyes to the value of acceptance without judgment. You have taught me lessons on how to coexist with my neighbors and how to share without expectations. You have given me comfort without words and love with your stares. You greet me as if I'm a surprise, each and every time; no matter how long I'm away from you. I feel secure with you.

So, it is with love I say the following: We all have idiosyncrasies; some are extremely noticeable, and some are not. Some are annoying and, of course, some are not.

It seems to me that we are not on the same sheet of music; you are constantly violating the rules. When I decided to have you come and stay with me, I spoke to you about unacceptable behaviors. I truly believed you understood; apparently not.

Let me finish, this is not the time to bark back.

On the issue of food, I provide you with the best food money can buy, yet, when we are having dinner you stare at my plate, especially when I'm having T-bone steak; it's as if you are starving. Do you ever see my cat . . . I mean your cousin Mime salivating at my plate? Stop! Show some decorum.

My plants— every single day I water them. Why do you

feel you have to water them too? And you pay special attention to the ones in the corners and along the fence, are you trying to kill them? I don't care if it's instinct; stay away from them! While we are on the subject of watering, what is the fascination you have with fire hydrants? They are public property and not to be used as a restroom.

You smell everything in your path. Don't you have any self-control? The way you smell the other dogs, it's embarrassing. Have you no home training?

When we go walking, you always walk in front of me. Why every five seconds do you have to look back? I find it annoying; I feel as if you are watching me for some unknown reason.

Last week I decided to take a bath instead of a shower. I filled the tub, went to make myself a drink, returned to the bathroom, and you were in the bathtub playing with my rubber duck! You crossed the line!

Do you have a clock in your head? Every day at the same time you find a reason to go to the gate. The mail carrier provides an important service; he is not to be harassed. If you are not satisfied living with me, explain. Don't just say, "Rough, rough!" I will not have this conversation with you again.

9.1.1.

Don Conway

The radio lit up, "Auto accident at Vermont Avenue and Wilshire Boulevard" the Dispatcher's voice came through the speaker.

"Unit six responding," the EMT said into the microphone.

The location of the accident was quickly typed into the ambulance's control panel followed by the letters A1. The driverless ambulance, reacting to the A1 code, turned on its flashing lights and siren, did a U-turn and headed for the site of the accident.

Unit six was the first to arrive at the scene. What they saw was a compact car with a crushed-in roof. The roof was entirely flattened. There was steam coming out of the engine compartment and gasoline dripping from the rear of the small car.

"Looks like it rolled over a couple of times."

"I agree. Lucky for us it landed on its wheels. We should be able to get into it."

"Let's take a look inside first."

"Uh-oh, there's a young girl in there."

"Jaws of life for sure."

"I'll get em." He ran back to the ambulance to get the giant cutting tool.

"Okay, I'll cut, but you need to stand between me and that gasoline to block the sparks. One spark from the jaws and we will all have had it."

It took eight minutes to cut the roof off the car. Together the EMT's lifted the unconscious girl out of the car and placed her on the stretcher. They began to examine her.

"I've got a compound fracture of the right femur here. Tourniquet going on now, just in case the artery breaks." he said.
"Vital signs are all weak but there is still a heartbeat," the other said. "She's gasping for air. Probably a collapsed lung. Oxygen mask and air on." He reported.

"Okay, that's all we can do to stabilize her for now. Let's head to the hospital."

They loaded the stretcher into the ambulance and typed in the code for St.Vincent's hospital followed by the A1 code. With lights flashing and sirens, blaring the driverless ambulance sped off to the hospital. En route, one of the technicians typed in the information on the girl's condition. When they got to the emergency entrance of the hospital, there were an ER nurse and two orderlies waiting for them. The girl was quickly transferred to a gurney and rushed to a waiting doctor."I'll go to the supply room and replenish what we've used," one EMT said.

"Okay, I'll clean up the inside of the ambulance while you do that," the other EMT offered. Outside of the Emergency room, the two orderlies stopped for a smoke. "Man, that was close," George said.

"Yeah, I didn't think she was going to make it," Emelio replied. "Damn, but those EMT's are good!"

"You got that right. When they first brought in those EMT robots I didn't think they would work out but those two sure proved me wrong."

WHY CAN'T PEOPLE GET ALONG?

Jim Wiggins

Why can't people get along?
It seems so wrong, wrong, wrong.
Can't we love our brother and have respect for one another?
It seems so wrong, wrong, wrong.

Why do people hate? Is this our fate?
It seems so wrong, wrong, wrong.
Men dying in trenches because of war's consequences.
It seems so wrong,wrong,wrong.

Why is there so much hatred? Does nothing remain sacred?
Must man live in fear of losing those he holds so dear?
Can we ever find calm and peace of mind?

Is there no refuge to be found?
Is there not enough love to go around?

Will the violence never cease? Is there a path to find real peace?
Stupidity has gone on too long. It's wrong, wrong, wrong.

PEACE TRAIN

Virginia Guido

"Come on, we're gonna be late!" Pulling Miranda along the platform of the train station, I could tell that Miranda (Randy for short) was still hesitant about this trip. But I had persuaded her and guaranteed that it would be fun. "After all, YOLO, you only live once," I had reminded Randy.

"A Murder Mystery Train ride, where the guests become part of the mystery? You can't refuse, Randy-girl."

"I don't like these things; they force me to act and put me on the spot."

"Don't be foolish. How can this be a bad thing? If you're not totally blown away by this trip, I promise, next time, we'll do whatever safe and sound activity you like. I'll even give you back your ticket money."

"But it's a two day trip. That's a lot of time to spend on a train just for a show."

"And what did you have planned for that time? I can tell you- nothing- not- a- thing! Come on, girlfriend. We'll have a terrific time, I swear."

As we ran across the platform, I shouted to Randy, one more time, "Come on, hurry! I don't want to be late."

Fortunately, we made it to the train with enough time to check our bags. The outside of the train was painted black and looked foreboding. *It must be part of the show*, I figured. The writing along each car was Gothic and read DEATH TRAIN. *Well there's no mystery there, huh?*

As we entered the reception car, we were greeted by an elderly man in a tuxedo who offered us drinks from a silver tray. Neither one of us took a glass. We had our own water bottles, and it was too early in the day to imbibe.

"What's in the glass, anyway?" I asked the disappointed waiter.

"It's the Death Train's signature drink. I do wish you'd have some--to toast your journey."

"Nah, we'll wait for the show tonight before we start drinking."

"Show?" He seemed confused."Yes, of course, the show tonight. By the way, the dining car will be serving dinner in one hour."

Too excited to be hungry, we went to the club car to relax and mingle with our fellow travelers. As we watched the scenery glide by the window, dozens of passengers, actors and non actors, I guess, also settled in the car. Conversation built up to a blaring pitch.

But our attention was pulled to a couple, three tables away from us. They were coughing loudly enough to be heard over the din of the conversations.

Realization hit me. They weren't coughing; they were choking, gagging, and frothing at the mouth. Randy and I were the only ones watching them as everyone else went about their business. *What kind of murder mystery is this, with no reaction to those two people? Shouldn't we at least feign surprise or pretend to help?*

As the couple finally stopped writhing and slumped over the table, our colleagues raised their own glasses to toast their departure. This bizarre act was followed by another group of passengers, at the other end of the car, coughing and choking. I looked at Randy in disbelief. "What the hell is going on?" I said, under my breath.

We nonchalantly got up from our booth, each holding a glass, making it appear as if we were drinking too, and exited the car. Still, this maneuver did not guarantee our safety. Walking through the next car, we observed several passengers slouched over the burgundy seats. Some seemed to be sleeping, but we knew better.

"Let's find our berth." I whispered. "We need to speak in private."

Randy and I struggled to look nonplussed as we edged our way to the sleeping cars. There was an eerie silence inside the train, accompanied by the hypnotic sound of metal on metal outside.

It sounded like **"Can't turn back. Can't turn back. Can't turn back."** I don't know what was happening at the time, but I certainly knew I was not paranoid. Something was wrong, very wrong.

In the privacy of our berth, Randy and I discussed what we thought was transpiring. This was not a murder mystery train ride at all; this was a suicide convoy streaking to hell.

"We have to get off," I said.

"How? Are we going to jump?"

"No, I'll pull the emergency cord. The train has to stop. Then we'll slip out between the cars and jump. It's our only way to escape. Look, I'll do it now. We're about to approach a stockyard. We can get help there."

Outside our berth, both of us inched as close to the end of the car as possible, and I pulled the cord nearest the door. The shrieking sound of the train braking scraped through our brains as the car slowed down. We opened the door and came face-to-face with the elderly waiter, still carrying his tray.

"You can't leave! You have to stay until you reach your final destination."

"That's what you think, old man! Get out of our way!" I pushed him aside and leapt off the platform on to the brush, surrounding the tracks.

Randy was about to jump when the old man grabbed her. Suddenly, he looked taller; his tuxedo had turned into a black hooded robe, and the tray became a scythe. Randy screamed as he enveloped her, and the train picked up speed again.

It disappeared from my sight and I have a feeling that it's never coming back… and neither is Randy.

GUN CONTROL

John F. Rifenberg

Now, I'm the hunter, brave and true, and this is my trusty gun.
I hunt wild rabbits, ducks and geese and kill them just for fun.
Those armor piercing, Teflon- coated bullets are the best.
Especially for shooting those squirrels who wear bullet-proof vests.

Now, I'm in the NRA, an honorable man.
Defending the amendments rights as a good American can.
Without the right to carry arms, we wouldn't stand a chance.
And then there's all the stock I own in ammunitions plants.

Now, I'm in the Senate and I'm nobody's fool.
I'm tough and independent, no special interest tool.
Now, I believe in gun control, but all you need to know.
The NRA is the group that gives me my campaign dough.

Now, I was toilet trained at 23 'because I was insecure.
I'm a paranoid schizophrenic with delusions of grandeur.
They locked me up because I waved my pee-pee at a nun.
But, though I cannot drive or vote, I still can buy a gun!

So, if you're the one who takes up the gun.
From the mantelpiece or shelf.
Eliminate the middle man and shoot your fucking self!

THE CLOSET

Hartley Barnes

So, this marriage thing is about sharing equally on all fronts. A good idea by whoever thought it up, except for, the woman, her clothes, and her shoes. My wife and I started out with equal rights to the walk-in closet. I could walk in and browse along my thirty feet, find what I want, and move on—with no problem, the same for her.

Closet space is not something I dwell on; it's there, and it serves a purpose, but I started to notice my area getting smaller. My wife, Elane, is encroaching on my space without a hint of compassion for my needs. I complain, and her response is, "You have things in there you don't wear, get rid of them. Of course, I agree, not realizing she's making more room for her stuff. How clever.

Over the years I've seen my portion of the closet dwindle to a corner less than two feet. Elane goes in the closet, and it's a shopping spree. For me, it's a hunting trip with frustration. All my shoes have been relegated to the garage and replaced with hers, many still in the box they came in, and have never been worn. Her inventory reminds me of Imelda Marcos. I have four or five garments on one hanger, and it's repeated over and over. I have to excavate the closet to get my clothes.

I recently met with some friends at a nearby sports bar. I was rushed for time; I went to the closet and started digging where

I last saw my clothes. I found a pair of jeans and hurriedly put them on. They didn't feel comfortable; I thought maybe I washed them in hot water and they shrank a little.

So, I get to where I'm going, and the jeans are still uncomfortable. I go to the bar and take a seat. There is a mirror behind the display of bottles and a large mirror on the wall across from the bar. As I ordered my drink, I could see my back in the mirror to my front. What stood out were the letters P-I-N-K on the back of the jeans I'm wearing. That explains why I'm getting all these intense stares, especially from the women. I canceled the drink and exited the bar as graciously as I possibly could by walking backwards. I rushed home, not feeling myself.

Coming through the front door, Elane is in the living room, no greetings, nothing, except a horrified look. "You're wearing my clothes now? Does this mean you like . . . "

"NO! Don't befacetious, this is your fault. If I could go into the closet and not feel like I'm going on a hunting trip, I wouldn't make a mistake and wear your clothes. I can't see my stuff in there anymore." *I'm feeling deflated.* "I'm sorry I'm not feeling macho. Damn it! PINK! Why not blue, red, or even yellow? If you tell anyone about this, I'll go see my lawyer."

"Oh, stop the noise," she laughingly said to me. "Did you feel sexy?"

All I could say is, "Okay, okay," while taking a deep breath. "I want my closet space back."

Playfully, she responded, "I'm sorry, Turnip, I can't help you."

"Why not?"

"It's in our contract. You didn't read the fine print."

"This must be April Fool's Day. What contract?"

"Come, I'll show you." We go upstairs to the bedroom.

"I don't recall seeing a contract."

"You were drunk."

How convenient. She goes to the nightstand on her side of the bed and takes some papers from its drawer. "Here, last page, last paragraph."

I looked at the page, "I can't see this writing Elane." She hands me a magnifying glass with a huge smile on her face.

"Closet space is contingent on how many clothes the wife has and is subject to change as the years pass in her favor."

"You've got to be joking. I don't recollect ever seeing this."

"I'm sure you saw it. Anyway, I'm going to New York on a business trip in a couple of days. Will you be okay alone? "

"Yeah, I'm suddenly feeling very energetic; spring is almost here— I'll do some cleaning up. When you get back, I'll take you out to dinner. Buy something to wear."

Elane returns. She's upbeat. I told her to get cleaned up, and we'll go out. She goes up to the bedroom, and ten seconds later there is a mind-blowing scream. She rushes down the stairs. "Where are my clothes? Where are my clothes? Call 911!"

"Calm down, honey, there's no point getting hysterical; it's only clothes."

"Don't tell me to calm down! Where are my clothes?"

"You didn't read the fine print on the reverse side of the last page of our contract, dear."

"There is no contract!"

"Yes, sweetie, there is. I found my copy. It says, "'However, if the husband feels the wife is being selfish, he can take his closet space back. The Salvation Army is so grateful for your large donation, my Sweet Corn.'"

THE ARTIST'S HEADACHE

Richard Paul Angelini

"Art Is The Lie That Helps Us Realize The Truth"

- Pablo Picasso

Picasso had it right. Or, maybe left. Think of his cubist period. I like to remember the chick with the nose to the right, or was it to the left? Could it be she squirmed? I mean, just a little; and to the right, (or left)?

Or, could he have been distracted? Did he paint a bust of her and not her bust, (specifically, to the belly button), and not risk loosing the inspiration that is art?

Perhaps she was an intermittent model. One with other chores. Chores that drew her away from the studio again and again. Did Picasso become frustrated trying to paint a beautiful woman who kept changing mood with experiences outside the studio; and returned each time with different emotional complexes to be explored by the artist? Fleeting emotions that ran across the canvass and were gone?

Then too, perhaps it was the bust, (knowing Picasso's reputation). Still, Picasso painted and maybe realized the truth. Or maybe not.

In cubism he liberally shared the artist's headache of the

changing canvass. For that we should be thankful, (I guess).

Sometimes I like to sit alone in darkness and just laugh...

FINALLY

Donna S. Fernandez

We need rain in sunny South Florida
no matter how the tourists scoff at this
being *their holiday and all*. Those who
witness the bloom, the buzz, the birth,
the chirp while canals gasp under a
relentless sun drying and lowering its
water's edge, but continues to give
new life bound for suffocating beings.
Breath in.
Breath out.
Rain falls.
Life-giving rain.

AUTHORS

Richard Paul, (Rick) Angelini, a retired school teacher, came to Florida in 1959 and has many stories to tell. His published novel, The Christmas Bike, set in 1959 Florida, is told from a 10 year old kid's point of view. His wife, Vicki, is his greatest fan. They have two married children and their first grandchild, Louie.

Hartley Barnes is a veteran who has served in three wars: Vietnam, Desert Storm and Iraqi Freedom. Retired from te Army in 2006, and went to work in Iraq and Afghanistan as a civilian contractor for six years. He is now home and writing. his focuses are creative and playwriting.

Margie Bonner was born and raised in Canada. Her professional career includes thirty years at JFK Hospital, working as a nurse. She considers the art of writing a true gift. For her, a novice writer, it is the joy of the journey. She is one of the original founders of the Writing Group of Royal Palm Beach.

Don Conway, Prof. Emeritus got hooked on storytelling and writing in 2012. The Veterans Administration awarded him a Gold Medal in 2014 and Gold and Silver Medals in 2015 for his entries in the VA's National Creative Arts Competition. The RPWG is his go-to family/support group.

Karina G. Felix was born and raised in Aruba. She is the founder of Ingenious Publishers Inc, the publishing house for *DANZ'N*

Magazine, *Infinite Lifestyle Magazi*ne and the 14th edition of *Spectrum*. She lives in Royal Palm Beach with her children Sergio and Kiara and their three dogs, Diva, Phoenix and Luna.

Donna S. Fernandez lives in Wellington. As a writer, she is a reader. Behind Donna's home is a tropical garden, more akin to a botanical masterpiece. This Eden is the source for many "reads and writes," and on the best reading and writing days, the pages fly.

Gloria Ferrara enjoys writing about times spent with family and friends she left moving to Florida in 1985. Through her stories, she renews experiences shared with them. This year's Spectrum includes her story "Relationship Broken". She is one of the original founders of the Writing Group of Royal Palm Beach.

Virginia Guido is a retired NYC school administrator, living in Florida. She is married to Ralph, her childhood sweetheart, for 43 years. Her twin daughters (Natalie and Paulette) produced grandsons (Jax, Gio, and Jet) and a princess granddaughter (Bianca). Her son, Frankie, died in 2008. Virginia likes writing memoirs about her eccentric past. The Writing Group/Family is her therapeutic support.

Dorothy M. Littlefield is the author of Journey into the Land of the Wingless Giants, her first published novel. She enjoys writing humorous stories, romance, mysteries, and fairytales. She lived in Kilgore, Texas, and raised horses before she moved to West Palm Beach, Florida, to be near her daughter.

Judith Ann Pelio was born and raised in New York City and presently lives in Wellington, Florida. She has a Business Degree from

New York University and a Master's Degree in Psychology from New York Institute of Technology. Judy enjoys writing emotionally-charged poetry, memoirs, and essays. She is currently writing a book dedicated to and in honor of her recently passed twin sister.

John F. Rifenberg lives in Royal Palm Beach, Florida with his vivacious and loving wife, Frankie, who supports his radical view of the solar system; in which Florida is the center of the universe, and Boca Raton is the capital. He is looking forward to the Beatles reuniting, peace on earth, and lower gas prices.

Virginia (Ginny) Smythe is a recovering workaholic that escaped corporate America. She moved to the Acreage from Maryland eleven years ago and has not looked back. Writing is her newest creative outlet, but she also has an entire room in her house dedicated to her sewing/embroidery hobby. She is a happy go lucky kind of gal with a house full of dogs and plays a serious game of poker.

Shanda Whittle is a Buffalo native who went to school in Maine to become a nurse. She is enjoying her snowless days here in Florida with the Royal Palm Beach Writers group, aspiring towards her first-grade dream of becoming a book technician, AKA, a writer.

Jim Wiggins is a fourth generation Floridian. He and his wife, Colleen, live in The Acreage. They have eleven grandchildren and five great-grandchildren. Two of their four children are deceased. Jim has published numerous articles in magazines and is currently the author of thirteen books.

www.ingramcontent.com/pod-product-compliance
Lightning Source LLC
Chambersburg PA
CBHW050303110726
47898CB00007B/2522

* 9 7 8 1 7 3 2 9 6 9 6 0 5 *